book *of* faith
Lenten Journey

D0711906

book *of* faith
Lenten Journey
Beyond Question

Eric Burtness

BOOK OF FAITH LENTEN JOURNEY
Beyond Question

References to ELW are from *Evangelical Lutheran Worship* (Augsburg Fortress, 2006).

Text on pages 7–18 adapted from David L. Miller, *Book of Faith Lenten Journey: Marks of the Christian*
(Augsburg Fortress, 2009); Henry F. French, *Book of Faith Lenten Journey: 40 Days with the Lord's Prayer*
(Augsburg Fortress, 2009); and Ron Klug, *How to Keep a Spiritual Journal* (Augsburg Books, 1993).

For information on the Book of Faith initiative and Book of Faith resources, go to www.bookoffaith.org.

Book of Faith is an initiative of the

Evangelical Lutheran Church in America
God's work. Our hands.

Cover design: David Meyer
Interior design: Ivy Palmer Skrade
Typesetting: PerfecType, Nashville, TN

ISBN 978-1-4514-2389-1

Manufactured in the U.S.A.

Contents

Our Writer

Eric Burtness is the lead pastor at Zion Lutheran Church in Redmond, Oregon. He has served as pastor of large and small congregations in Minnesota, Wisconsin, and Oregon. He is the author of *Leading On Purpose* (2004) and *A Life Worth Leading* (2006), both from Augsburg Fortress.

Book of Faith Lenten Journey: Beyond Question is dedicated to the memory of Eric's father, Jim Burtness (1928–2006), who taught at Luther Seminary, St. Paul, Minnesota, for more than forty years. Jim's inquisitive and questioning mind helped thousands of people understand more deeply what they believe to be true about faith and life.

Preface

The Book of Faith Initiative of the Evangelical Lutheran Church in America (ELCA) affirms the centrality of the Bible to Christian life and faith, while at the same time seeking to address the lack of biblical knowledge and engagement in many parts of our church.

The purpose of the Book of Faith Initiative is to increase biblical literacy and fluency for the sake of the world. The ELCA has made a commitment to encourage all members of congregations, from children to adults, to dig deeper into our book of faith, the Bible. The Book of Faith Initiative recommends a new model for our church: a grassroots approach embracing a common vision in which all are invited to open Scripture and join the conversation. Each community is encouraged to decide how the Book of Faith Initiative will become a vital part of its own ministry. Be sure to visit the Book of Faith Web site (www.bookoffaith. org) for other resources designed to bring the book of faith and the community of faith closer together.

As the language of the Bible becomes more and more our native tongue, it will continually shape how we think and speak about God, about the world, and about ourselves. As we immerse ourselves in Scripture, Christ, the incarnate Word of God and center of our faith, is birthed within us. The Bible tells the stories of people living their faith over the centuries and, through its demands and promises, forms us as a people of faith. We become renewed, enlivened, empowered, and transformed as God, through Scripture, forms hearts, minds, and conversations.

Book of Faith Lenten Journey: Beyond Question has been written to help you, in your own context, live into the commitments of the initiative and accomplish our common purpose. This book will engage you in an encounter with the living and active power of the Word of God. Each week the journey uses passages from Scripture to explore the questions of Jesus.

You can use *Book of Faith Lenten Journey: Beyond Question* on your own or with your family, a spiritual friend or small group, or your entire congregation. Related worship helps and sermon starters for midweek Lenten worship are available online at www.augsburgfortress.org. (Search for the title *Beyond Question*. Click on the title and then open the "Worship Helps" tab in the product description.)

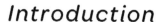

Introduction

Welcome to *Beyond Question*, a transformative journey through Lent. Throughout the Gospels, Jesus uses questions to change the lives and deepen the discipleship of those who follow him. In this book of Lenten devotions, you are invited to open Scripture and encounter Jesus and his transformative questions.

Jesus does not ask questions to get simple answers from us or to give simple answers to us. In fact, Jesus only directly answers three of the 186 questions addressed to him in the Gospels and often answers a question with a question of his own. Nor is the task of the church to give simple answers to complex questions. Rather, it is to ask empowering questions that draw people into a deeper understanding of their own faith and discipleship. Jesus asks these kinds of questions—questions that reposition us, challenge our images of God and our place in the world, and present us with new and creative possibilities for transformation. He asks probing, realigning, transformative questions to change core convictions and motivate new behaviors.

The quality of the questions determines the quality of the answers. Limiting questions can only provide us with limited answers—the same old unhelpful answers that often just drag us down instead of draw us out. Jesus' empowering questions lead us to empowered answers. They shift our perspective to new and fresh ways of looking at and solving our problems or issues. These empowering questions affect the quality of our lives and deepen our faith and discipleship.

This book invites you on a journey into deeper discipleship as each week we focus on one key question of Jesus.

- What are you looking for? (Week One)
- Where is your faith? (Week Two)
- Who do you say that I am? (Week Three)

- What do you want me to do for you? (Week Four)
- Do you love me? (Week Five)
- How will you believe what I say? (Week Six)
- Whom are you looking for? (Week Seven)

These questions will encourage and challenge you to examine your priorities and faith, consider who Christ is, define and articulate your beliefs about faith and life, and grow as a faithful follower of Jesus.

Questions like "Who do you say that I am?" are not questions that call for quick and simple answers, so allow yourself to *live with the questions* on this journey. Some of Jesus' questions may linger with you for days, weeks, years, or throughout the rest of your life. You might find you're not ready to answer some of the questions at this time. Maybe one or two of the questions will trigger other questions for you. Consider keeping a journal as you ponder Jesus' questions, pray about them, wrestle with them, contemplate answers, reconsider your responses, leave some questions for another time, discuss questions with others, and ask your own questions. Live with the questions of Jesus as you take this forty-day journey of transformation and discipleship.

Praying the Scriptures

Martin Luther's barber, Peter, asked him how an ordinary person should pray. In response, Luther wrote *A Simple Way to Pray*, in which he encouraged Christians to pray in their own words, rather than reciting prayers they had memorized, and to trust the Holy Spirit to guide them.

Christians today typically have more experience with personal prayer than did the ordinary men and women of Luther's day, who would have known only the Our Father, the Hail Mary, and a few other prayers heard at mass or taught for private devotion. Even for us, though, it is easy to feel uncomfortable and inadequate with our praying. Luther's advice to Peter offers us a simple, concrete way to enter more deeply and personally into prayer. He suggested starting with a text—from Scripture, the catechism, or other devotional material such as hymns—and reading it in four ways:

- Read it as a schoolbook, reflecting upon what God is teaching you.
- Read it as a song or praise book, giving thanks to God for the gifts God gives or brings to your awareness.
- Read it as a penitential book, confessing to God your sins, your needs, and your weaknesses as they are revealed in your reflection.
- Turn the words into a short prayer you speak to God.

There are no right or wrong prayers in this approach. Luther's intent was that our hearts would be stirred and guided.

Luther's core conviction is that the Scriptures are not intended to fill our heads with interesting ideas, but to bring the transformative power of God's Word into our lives. Bible study and prayer belong together. Worship is also a part of this dynamic encounter. Christians through the ages have recognized that what we believe shapes how we worship and also that how we worship shapes what we believe. Both, in turn, guide how we behave. Over time, what we say, do, sing, hear, and experience in worship influences us and forms our faith. For this reason Luther did not stop with translating the Scriptures into German. He also translated the worship service into the language of the people. He incorporated congregational singing into the liturgy and composed new hymns to teach the Christian faith through song. You will notice references to songs or hymns woven into this Lenten journey.

As you embark on this forty-day journey with Scripture and the questions of Jesus, you are invited most of all to come and follow him:

- Come prayerfully, asking the Holy Spirit to guide you and Christ to be with you.
- Come humbly, asking for the gifts of faith and renewal.
- Come mindfully, bringing to your study the gifts of reason, the tools of scholarship, and the insights of others.
- Come attentively, reading Scripture carefully and closely.
- Come collectively, in the context of faithful community, letting your own stories interact with the stories of the Bible.

- Come expectantly, listening for the voice of God working through the texts to inspire, shape, and enliven you individually and in your community of faith.

"Do not be conformed to this world, but be transformed by the renewing of your minds, so that you may discern what is the will of God—what is good and acceptable and perfect" (Romans 12:2).

How to Use This Book

This forty-day Lenten journey explores many of the questions Jesus used to deepen discipleship. The journey will encourage you to think, pray, and reflect on how these questions might lead and guide you into new paths of discovery. You will come to ponder *why you believe what you believe*, and you will be both challenged and strengthened throughout this journey.

It will help if you pay close attention to what God is saying to you, asking of you, confirming in you, and working in you. This journey will get at the heart of what Jesus is asking, not just seeking simple answers, but wrestling with the questions and helping you exercise your faith through conversation and prayer. In this way, your personal discipleship will grow and deepen as you discover ways your faith can be affirmed and strengthened.

It is often easier to maintain a spiritual practice if you do it regularly, at the same time each day. For many people, morning, while the house is still quiet and before the busyness of the day begins, is a good time. Others will find that the noon hour or before bedtime serves well. If you are working through this book with a partner, a group, or as family devotions, you might gather in the morning or before or after a meal. Do whatever works for you to maintain a regular, daily encounter with God.

You will note that there are no readings for Sunday. The forty days of Lent traditionally exclude Sundays, the days we celebrate the resurrection of Christ.

Although this book is designed to be used during Lent, it can be used at any time of the year. If you pick a time other than Lent for your journey, it will still be best to walk day by day through the book. Each day's devotion offers rich resources for you to ponder. There is no need to rush, so feel free to slow down and take more than forty days with this material. It is better to complete the journey at your own pace than to give it up partway through. Set a schedule that works for you, and be as consistent as you can.

The amount of time you spend in devotions each day is entirely up to you. Sometimes you may only have a few minutes. Sometimes you might find it fruitful to spend more than one day with a particular reflection, question, or quotation that stirs you. If one element speaks more deeply to you than others, spend time with it. Always go where there is fruit and discovery. Don't worry that the other elements don't touch your mind or heart that day. Go where Jesus is speaking to you and giving himself to you. Luther wrote, "If you pause here and let him do you good, that is if you believe that he benefits and helps you, then you really have it. The Christ is yours, presented to you as a gift."[1]

The Daily Plan

Each day of the journey begins with a question that Jesus asked as a way to draw out what was in the heart of the hearer and deepen faith and discipleship. Following each question is a brief reflection intended to stir your own thinking and reflection. You may want to read through each question and reflection more than once, perhaps even reading these aloud so that you might hear the question and reflect on it, in addition to seeing it on the page. Let Jesus' question sink into your head and heart. Take time to ponder what Jesus is asking of you.

Following the daily reflection, you will find *Biblical Wisdom* and a brief passage from Scripture that relates to the meditation. It may be obvious to you how this second passage relates to the day's theme, or you may need to think about it for a while before you make the connection. Either way, read the Bible text slowly. Let it speak to you.

After this scriptural passage, you will find a *Transformative Thought*. This quotation from an author or speaker may lead you to think about the theme of the day in a different way or offer a word of encouragement on this transformative journey. Take time to dwell on this thought as well.

Next comes *Silence for Meditation*. You may already be steeped in a tradition of meditation involving getting centered, breathing slowly and deeply, focusing your attention, and taking time to be silent and listen. Or you may be uncomfortable with such practices. Just as public worship needs silence amid the prayer and song, so also does private devotion. So practice being still, listening within the silence, and quieting your mind and body. Silence leaves room for the Spirit to live and breathe and have its being. Think of silence as a time of refreshment; a time of re-spiriting, if you will.

Once you feel yourself settling down, slowly take a second look at the daily meditation, the Bible passages, and the Transformative Thought. Note the words, thoughts, images, and feelings that draw you. Explore meanings and implications for your life. Jot down any insights that occur to you. Do the readings raise additional questions for you? Do they suggest some action or response on your part? Write them down or discuss them with a devotional partner. Stay with the meditation time as long as it feels useful. When you are ready to move on, you might close your eyes, observe your breath for a minute, and thank God for the gifts of life and God's Word.

Then move on to the *Psalm Fragment*. The psalms are both our words to God and God's words to us. A mainstay of prayer for Jewish and Christian believers, they speak the deepest hope, joy, and pain of our lives. Read the Psalm Fragment silently or aloud, and reflect for a moment on how the psalm connects to the question of the day and moves you toward prayer.

In the section *Questions to Ponder* you will find questions related to the day's focus. These questions may be used for personal reflection, as a basis for conversation with others, or as journal prompts. Focus on the questions that draw you in and deepen your conversation with God and other people. Some questions may lead you to ask your own questions about faith and discipleship. Others may move you to further study or to some action steps. Go where the Spirit leads you.

The final section is *Prayer for Today*, which provides a brief prayer for ending your session. You might choose to repeat this prayer from time to time throughout the day. If you prefer, you can pray your own short prayer based on your time of reflection.

Keeping a Journal

Journaling as a spiritual practice can be profoundly transformative. It can keep you in touch with yourself and your response to God over time. Sometimes we really don't know or understand our thoughts and feelings until we write them down and see what we have written. We may be surprised at what is actually moving and happening in us. Then we can draw insight and consolation from what God is saying and doing.

Keeping a journal can also be a form of prayer, a powerful way of getting to know yourself—and God—more deeply. Journaling helps you focus and clarify your thoughts while keeping a record of your insights, questions, and prayers. It may lead you to thoughts and awareness that will surprise you. As you write, you can respond to God with your thanks and pleas, your joys and sorrows, offering them all to God.

Here are some hints for keeping a journal during this Lenten journey.

1. Write freely. Ignore your inner critic. Don't worry about grammar, literary style, whether you are writing in complete sentences, or what it sounds like. Just write! Simply get in touch with an idea, emotion, imagery, or memory and begin writing. Describe what you notice, how you feel, and how something is affecting you. From time to time, read back over your words to see more clearly what is happening.

2. Be honest with God. Do not censor yourself! Don't write what you think you're supposed to believe or feel or think. Don't write what you think is acceptable to your spouse or friends, your pastor, or your fourth-grade teacher. Write your real thoughts, feelings, beliefs, and experiences as best you can identify them. When you are uncertain, write your confusion and questions. Your relationship with God will be as real and honest as you are.

3. Begin and end your journaling with prayer. Ask for insight to see God's work more clearly, to notice what is really going on beneath the surface of your days and thoughts. At the end, thank God for what guidance, wisdom, or consolation has come through your writing.

4. Feel free to address God directly in your writing. You may choose to write your entire journal entry as a prayer. Share what is happening to you and in you, what you are noticing in your journey with this book. Like the psalmists and Job, hold nothing back. You may be surprised by what bubbles out of you.

5. Because this is a transformative journey through Lent, look for ways your thoughts or behaviors begin to reflect a deeper life of discipleship. At least once a week consider including action steps that reflect your commitment to a closer walk with Jesus. An action step might be as simple as a commitment to beginning or ending each day with a prayer of gratitude.

6. Don't worry or stop if your journaling takes you in directions beyond the suggestions in this book. Go where you are led. Notice what you notice. The Holy Spirit will lead you to places where you may drink from the living waters Christ Jesus offers. The journaling ideas and Questions to Ponder are suggestions for your writing. Don't hesitate to move in other directions when promising avenues appear.

7. You may wish to carry this book and your notebook or journal with you every day during your journey (but keep them safe from prying eyes). Your Lenten journey can be an intense experience that does not stop when you close the book. When your mind and heart are stirred during the day, it is helpful to be able to write notes or new journal entries as they occur to you.

Journeying with Others

You can use this book (and I hope you do) with a friend, family member, small group, or congregation. If you wish, each person can first do his or her own reading, reflection, and writing in solitude. When you come together, you can share the insights you have gained from your time alone. Your discussion can focus on any of the elements of each day's journey.

Questions to Ponder is a natural place to start discussion with a group or spiritual friend. However, you might find that a section from a daily reflection, Biblical Wisdom, or a Transformative Thought has particularly stirred one of you. If so, start there, and let the discussion flow in the directions that are most fruitful for your needs and questions. Trust that God's word will bear good fruit in your conversation.

If you are working through the book with people you trust, you may feel comfortable sharing some of what you have written in your journal. But no one should ever be pressured to do that. It should be a ground rule that whatever is said in a small group stays within the group.

Always remember that your goal is to grow in relationship with Christ and the church, and in your understanding of God's word. You gather to learn from one another, not to argue or to prove that you are right and the other is wrong. Practice listening and trying to understand why your discussion partner or small-group members think as they do.

Sharing your experiences is a way of encouraging and guiding one another. It provides you opportunity to offer feedback gently and to help one another translate insight into action.

By all means, pray with others. This strengthens the spiritual bonds among those who take the journey together. Spend a few moments sharing prayer requests around the theme of the day. Then pray for one another and your faith community as you bring your time together to a close.

Week One
What Are You Looking For?

Day 1—Ash Wednesday
What Are You Looking For?

John 1:35-42

> *The next day John again was standing with two of his disciples, and as*
> *he watched Jesus walk by, he exclaimed, "Look, here is the Lamb of God!"*
> *The two disciples heard him say this, and they followed Jesus. When*
> *Jesus turned and saw them following, he said to them, "What are you*
> *looking for?"*
>
> John 1:35-38a

Lent is a time of spiritual introspection. It's a time to pause in the midst of a very busy life, a challenging world, and a searching faith. Lent is a time to take a few moments regularly to think and reflect on Jesus, his journey to the cross, his death and resurrection, and what all of this means for our lives of faith.

Ash Wednesday is a time to pause, not to look forward to Easter and all the things that lie ahead, but to take things a bit more slowly and reflect on ourselves, our lives of faith, and the decisions we've made. Ash Wednesday is a day of repentance, turning from where we've been going and turning toward God. Ash Wednesday and Lent are the church's way of encouraging us to slow down, look at ourselves, and reflect on our faith and the meaning of our lives.

We begin this transformative journey through Lent with the first words Jesus speaks in the Gospel of John. Interestingly, Jesus' first words are not "Follow me." Nor are they, "I am the bread of life." Jesus' first words in John's Gospel come in the form of a question: "What are you looking for?" This is the same kind of searching question as the first one God asks in Genesis. God knew that Adam and Eve were hiding yet still asked, "Where are you?" (Genesis 3:9).

What are you looking for? What are you looking for as you begin this journey through Lent? How would you like this Lent to be different or more meaningful than previous Lenten seasons?

The ashes that many people receive on this day remind us that we are dust, and to dust we shall return. They remind us of our own frailty and utter dependence on God for life. Take time to pause this day and consider the cleansing and renewal you need in areas of your life. As you do this, remember that Jesus is one who is looking for you.

Biblical Wisdom
When you search for me, you will find me; if you seek me with all your heart, I will let you find me, says the Lord.
Jeremiah 29:13-14a

Transformative Thought
We have to keep looking for the spiritual questions if we want spiritual answers.[2]
Henri Nouwen

Silence for Meditation

Psalm Fragment
O Lord, you have searched me and known me.
Psalm 139:1

Questions to Ponder
- What are you looking for as you begin this journey through Lent? Where and when will you take time to pause and think about Jesus' life, death, and resurrection?
- If you received ashes on your forehead today or in the past, reflect on that experience. What areas of your life are in need of cleansing and renewal?

Prayer for Today
Gracious and loving God, be with me as I start this journey through Lent. Guide me into ways of deeper understanding and faith, that I might grow ever closer to you. Help me listen and help me grow. In Jesus' name. Amen.

Day 2—Thursday
Who Touched Me?
Luke 8:43-48

She came up behind him and touched the fringe of his clothes, and immediately her hemorrhage stopped. Then Jesus asked, "Who touched me?"
Luke 8:44-45a

The woman we read about in Luke 8 had a flow of blood for twelve years. Looking for healing, she had spent every last penny on doctors and treatments, but to no avail. Her condition just continued day after day, year after year. Can you imagine her frustration?

Even worse perhaps than her medical condition, her anemia, and her lack of energy, she was considered ritually unclean. This meant that anyone or anything she touched would become unclean, immediately contaminated. It was her religious duty to stay away from everyone and everything. She was socialized to believe that she was dirty, soiled, filthy, and untouchable.

What gave this person the courage to think her life could be different? Why didn't she just accept her place in life? Just who did this unclean, unworthy woman think she was?

Well, she was a child of God. And she had total confidence in Jesus' ability to change her life. She knew beyond a shadow of doubt that if she touched him, she would be made well.

She pressed through the crowds, this supposedly unclean, dirty, untouchable woman, passionate in the conviction that Jesus could bring her wholeness. She knew that Jesus was the answer to the questions she had been asking.

As she got near, she reached out and barely touched the fringe of Jesus' clothes. Immediately she was healed! Her flow of blood ceased. Her life was transformed.

"Who touched me?" Jesus asked. And when she came, trembling and falling down before him, she declared before everyone that she had touched him and was immediately healed. Jesus blessed her and told her that her faith in him had made her well.

Who did this unclean woman think she was? She was a child of God with utter confidence in Jesus' ability to heal, restore, forgive, and give new life, even when all of this seemed impossible.

Who was this unclean woman? Perhaps she was like you and me, each of us on this journey through Lent, seeking to come close and touch Jesus and receive the amazing healing and new life that only he can give.

Biblical Wisdom

That message spread throughout Judea, beginning in Galilee after the baptism that John announced: how God anointed Jesus of Nazareth with the Holy Spirit and with power; how he went about doing good and healing all who were oppressed by the devil, for God was with him.
    Acts 10:37-38

Transformative Thought

Dear Child of God, I write these words because we all experience sadness, we all come at times to despair, and we all lose hope that the suffering in our lives and in the world will ever end. I want to share with you my faith and my understanding that this suffering can be transformed and redeemed. There is no such thing as a totally hopeless case. Our God is an expert at dealing with chaos, with brokenness, with all the worst that we can imagine. God created order out of disorder, cosmos out of chaos, and God can do so always, can do so now—in our personal lives and in our lives as nations, globally. . . . Indeed, God is transforming the world now—through us—because God loves us.[3]
    Desmond Tutu

Silence for Meditation

Psalm Fragment

The Lord sustains them on their sickbed; in their illness you heal all their infirmities.
    Psalm 41:3

Questions to Ponder

- Think about a time you or someone you know experienced physical, emotional, or spiritual healing. What was that like?
- In Jesus' time some people were considered "unclean" or "unworthy." Although these labels aren't often used today, there are people who feel unclean or unworthy of Jesus' touch. What might you do to help someone like that?

Prayer for Today

Almighty and merciful God, reach into the depths of my heart and find those places where I feel unworthy or unclean. Bring me closer to you and touch me with your love, grace, and healing. In Jesus' name. Amen.

Day 3—Friday
What Can You Give in Return for Your Life?
Mark 8:34-37

"For what will it profit them to gain the whole world and forfeit their life? Indeed, what can they give in return for their life?"
Mark 8:36-37

Wouldn't it be tragic to climb the ladder of success only to realize, when you reached the top rung of that ladder, that it was leaned up against the wrong wall? Today's question from Jesus is about the deeper purpose or meaning of life and what God might want to do in and through you.

On Ash Wednesday we considered the question "What are you looking for?" As a pastor, I've found that many of us are looking for success, stability, relationships, health, and so on. But I've also found that deep down most of us are looking for a sense of meaning and purpose in our lives.

Most people approach life in one of three ways. The first approach might be called *survival*. Many people around the world live in survival mode, due to hunger, poverty, homelessness, unemployment, underemployment, or illness. Others in survival mode go to work, punch the clock, put in their time, and live for the weekend. Instead of saying, "Good morning, Lord," when they wake up each day, they say, "Good Lord, it's morning."

A second way we might approach life is *success*. In success mode, people work hard at succeeding at work, at home, or at school. They also live with the constant fear of failure and the nagging worry that no amount of success will ever be enough to be deeply satisfying.

A third approach is to live with *significance*. In this mode, you are becoming the person God created you to be and making a significant contribution in the lives of those around you and in the world. You know you are a child of the Most High God who knit you together in your mother's womb (Psalm 139:13). This God created you not merely to survive or succeed in the world's eyes, but to live a life of significance in relationship with God, others, and the world.

Success can be great. But it can also be fleeting. Jesus' question is an urgent call to not give up our lives in the pursuit of things that do not last. True significance comes from giving all that you are and all that you have to the care of Jesus, who loves you and wants you to grow in faith and know him more and more each day.

Biblical Wisdom

For surely I know the plans I have for you, says the Lord, plans for your welfare and not for harm, to give you a future with hope.
Jeremiah 29:11

Transformative Thought

Jesus came to announce to us that an identity based on success, popularity, and power is a false identity—an illusion! Loudly and clearly he says: "You are not what the world makes you; but you are children of God."[4]
Henri J. M. Nouwen

Silence for Meditation

Psalm Fragment
For it was you who formed my inward parts; you knit me together in my mother's womb.
Psalm 139:13

Questions to Ponder

- Which approach to life do you find yourself using most frequently: survival, success, or significance? How do you feel about this? What might you need to forfeit or give up to move toward living with significance?
- Consider saying this to yourself each day during this Lenten journey: *I am a child of God. I belong to God, believe in God, and will become the person God created me to be.*

Prayer for Today

Gracious God, you created me and all that exists, and have given me all things necessary for life. Thank you. Show me how to use my gifts to serve others nearby and around the world who are struggling to survive. Help me give all that I am and all that I have to you. This I ask in Jesus' name. Amen.

Day 4—Saturday
Do You Wish to Go Away?
John 6:51-69

Jesus asked the twelve, "Do you also wish to go away?"
John 6:67

One day Alice was walking along when she came to a fork in the road. While she was pondering which way to go, she saw the Cheshire Cat in a tree. "Which path should I take?" she asked. The Cheshire Cat replied, "That depends on where you want to go." Alice said, "I don't quite know where I want to go." The Cheshire Cat responded, "Then it doesn't matter which path you take."[5]

Today's question from Jesus comes at a turning point, a fork in the road, for those who are following him. Opposition to Jesus is beginning to escalate by this time in John's Gospel. And rather than just healing and performing miracles,

Jesus is now talking about sacrifice and "the hour" of his death. Then he says, "Those who eat my flesh and drink my blood abide in me, and I in them" (John 6:56).

The people following Jesus don't know if they want to go where he is now leading them. So they say, "This teaching is difficult; who can accept it?" (John 6:60). Something they don't like is beginning to happen. Jesus is starting down a path they are pretty sure they don't want to take. The Gospel reports that many people decided to turn back at this point.

"Do you also wish to go away?" Jesus then asks his twelve closest followers. And Peter replies, "Lord, to whom can we go? You have the words of eternal life. We have come to believe and know that you are the Holy One of God" (John 6:68-69).

Not all paths lead to the same destination, so it matters a great deal which ones you take. Maybe you are at a fork in the road and, for the first time in your life, want to truly follow Jesus wherever he goes. Maybe you have been on this path but experienced discipleship burnout or dropout somewhere along the way. Perhaps you are on a long-term break from faith, from church, or from following Jesus, because it just got too difficult or unfulfilling. Wherever you have been, wherever you are now, Jesus, the Holy One of God, calls you to follow him and to keep following—all the way to the cross.

Biblical Wisdom

So if you have been raised with Christ, seek the things that are above, where Christ is, seated at the right hand of God.
Colossians 3:1

Transformative Thought

Go where thou wilt, seek what thou wilt, and thou shalt not find a higher way above, nor a safer way below, than the way of the holy Cross.[6]
Thomas à Kempis

Silence for Meditation

Psalm Fragment
Your word is a lamp to my feet and a light to my path.
   Psalm 119:105

Questions to Ponder

- Think back on a time you were lost, on the circumstances, how you felt, and how you finally found your way. What did you learn from this experience?
- Many people decided to turn back rather than continue on with Jesus. What holds you back from following Jesus, no matter where the path leads? What helps you stay on this path?

Prayer for Today

Holy God, our strength and our redeemer, by your Spirit hold us forever, that through your grace we may worship you and faithfully serve you, follow you and joyfully find you, through Jesus Christ, our Savior and Lord. Amen.[7]

Day 5—Monday
Do You Want to Be Made Well?
   John 5:2-9a

One man was there who had been ill for thirty-eight years. When Jesus saw him lying there and knew that he had been there a long time, he said to him, "Do you want to be made well?"
   John 5:5-6

Susan had hit bottom.

Her life was a mess. She just couldn't give up drinking. She craved alcohol from the moment she woke up until she passed out at night.

Day after day the cycle continued and worsened. She started hiding a bottle under the front seat of her car. She started missing work because she was too hung over to show up. As time went on, she lost her job, which resulted in more drinking. Her husband, sick and tired of her drinking and inability to quit, divorced her. Susan drove home after a party one evening and was arrested for driving under the influence. She lost custody of her children. With no income, she started forging checks. After she was arrested for check fraud, Susan realized she had hit bottom but was still digging.

In her growing despair, Susan asked herself, "Why can't I quit drinking? Why is this happening to me? Why don't people just leave me alone?" Finally she realized that those dead-end questions weren't getting her anywhere.

So she started asking herself, "What can I do to avoid drinking this morning? This afternoon? This evening? How can I keep sober, just one day at a time?" After several failed attempts, she managed one day of recovery. Then two. Then a week. She went to ninety Alcoholics Anonymous meetings in ninety days. Finally, she was able to turn her will and her life over to God's care. With God's help, the downward spiral of her life was reversed. Susan's entire life started to change for the better.

Susan changed her questions. By changing her questions, she changed her life. One day at a time.

"Do you want to be made well?" The answer seems so obvious to us; why would Jesus even bother to ask? The man had been ill for a long time, in fact, very ill for thirty-eight years. But Jesus asked the question and started a conversation with the man. And more than physical healing, the man received wholeness and restoration too.

Truth be told, each of us is wounded and in need of healing in some way. Do you want to be made well? Jesus can provide strength and healing—and even more—to overcome your wounds.

Biblical Wisdom
Cast all your anxiety on him, because he cares for you.
   1 Peter 5:7

Transformative Thought
I need to concentrate not so much on what needs to be changed in the world as on what needs to be changed in me and in my attitudes.[8]
   Bill Wilson

Silence for Meditation

Psalm Fragment
Create in me a clean heart, O God, and put a new and right spirit within me.
Psalm 51:10

Questions to Ponder
- What kind of questions do you ask yourself that immobilize you or don't lead you anywhere? What kinds of questions can you ask yourself that will have positive results in your life?
- In what ways do you want Jesus to make you well?

Prayer for Today
God, grant me the serenity to accept the things I cannot change; courage to change the things I can; and wisdom to know the difference. Amen.[9]

Day 6—Tuesday
Whom Are You Looking For?
John 18:1-8

Now Judas, who betrayed him, also knew the place, because Jesus often met there with his disciples. So Judas brought a detachment of soldiers together with police from the chief priests and the Pharisees, and they came there with lanterns and torches and weapons. Then Jesus, knowing all that was to happen to him, came forward and asked them, "Whom are you looking for?"
John 18:2-4

We began this Lenten journey on Ash Wednesday with the first words that Jesus speaks in John's Gospel, "What are you looking for?" We end our first week with the last words Jesus speaks before his betrayal and arrest.

What are you looking for? *Whom* are you looking for? Between those two questions lies Jesus' entire public ministry in the Gospel of John. They are the bookends for Jesus' ministry in the Gospel, and the bookends of our first week.

Jesus was in the Garden of Gethsemane when Judas arrived with a detachment of soldiers and police carrying lanterns, torches, and weapons. Jesus stepped forward and asked them, "Whom are you looking for?" They said, "Jesus of Nazareth," and he replied, "I am he." They stepped back and fell to the ground at his response. He asked a second time, "Whom are you looking for?" After this they arrested him, bound him, and brought him to trial.

The question "Whom are you looking for?" brought him death.

A few days later, Mary went to the tomb of Jesus. Devastated after his crucifixion and death, tears were streaming down her face. She wasn't able to see or recognize Jesus, now raised from the dead. She had no idea that the one standing right in front of her was exactly the one she was looking for. Jesus asked her, "Woman, why are you weeping? Whom are you looking for?" (John 20:15). When he spoke her name, she recognized him, and her tears of sorrow turned into tears of joy.

The question "Whom are you looking for?" brought her life.

Lent is a time to pause and turn and face Jesus, who calls you by name and invites you into a deeper relationship with him. Whom are you looking for?

Biblical Wisdom
From there you will seek the Lord your God, and you will find him if you search after him with all your heart and soul.
    Deuteronomy 4:29

Transformative Thought
I wonder whether I have sufficiently realized that during all this time God has been trying to find me, to know me, and to love me. The question is not "How am I to find God?" but "How am I to let myself be found by him?" The question is not "How am I to know God?" but "How am I to let myself be known by God?" And, finally, the question is not "How am I to love God?" but "How am I to let myself be loved by God?" God is looking into the distance for me, trying to find me, and longing to bring me home.[10]
Henri J. M. Nouwen

Silence for Meditation

Psalm Fragment
For you have delivered my soul from death, and my feet from falling, so that I may walk before God in the light of life.
    Psalm 56:13

Questions to Ponder

- What do you think about Jesus' questioning of the soldiers and police in the Garden of Gethsemane? Who was in charge there?
- What or who did you look for in the past? What or who are you looking for now?

Prayer for Today
Lord Jesus, you call me by name and invite me into a deeper relationship with you. Guide me and teach me on this walk with you. In your holy name. Amen.

Week Two
Where Is Your Faith?

Day 7—Wednesday
Where Is Your Faith?
Luke 8:22-25

> *A windstorm swept down on the lake, and the boat was filling with water, and they were in danger. They went to him and woke him up, shouting, "Master, Master, we are perishing!" And he woke up and rebuked the wind and the raging waves; they ceased, and there was a calm. He said to them, "Where is your faith?"*
> Luke 8:23b-25a

A friend of mine took a series of classes to learn how to drive Indy race cars. Really fast race cars. The instructor told him, "The most important thing for you to remember is how to come out of a skid when you're driving 150 miles an hour. When they start to skid, most people focus on what they fear most—crashing into the wall. Instead, you must focus on where you want to go." In a race-car skid, focusing on the problem doesn't help at all. Focusing on the solution guides you through a skid, because what you focus on is often where you'll end up.

Jesus' disciples were in a "boat skid," traveling across a lake during a huge storm. Terrified and in danger of sinking, they were focused on the wind and the waves. After they woke up Jesus, he spoke to the wind and waves, and they calmed down. Then Jesus asked the disciples, "Where is your faith?"

Many of us travel through life at 150 miles an hour, or at least it sometimes feels like that. At that speed, it's inevitable that we're going to skid at some point in our lives. And when we do, we ask questions like: "Why is this happening to me?" "Why can't I get my life together?" "Why don't my good intentions ever work out?" "Why can't I catch a break, just for once?" Instead of putting our faith in Jesus, we look for quick and easy solutions that don't help at all.

As the driving instructor said, stay focused on where you want to go. Always look to Jesus. Keep your eyes on him through the storms and skids of life. Put your faith in the one who will pull you through.

Biblical Wisdom
"Come to me, all you that are weary and are carrying heavy burdens,
and I will give you rest."
　　Matthew 11:28

Transformative Thought
The terrible thing, the almost impossible thing, is to hand over your whole self—all your wishes and precautions—to Christ. But it is far easier than what we are all trying to do instead. For what we are trying to do is to remain what we call "ourselves," to keep personal happiness as our great aim in life, and yet at the same time be "good."[11]
　　C. S. Lewis

Silence for Meditation

Psalm Fragment
He made the storm be still, and the waves of the sea were hushed.
　　Psalm 107:29

Questions to Ponder
- Think about a difficult situation in your life that had a positive outcome. What or who pulled you through that difficult time?
- What or who do you rely on most? Where do you put your faith?

Prayer for Today
God of power and might, calm my storms, calm my mind, and calm my spirit. Let me find rest in you. Ease my anxiety, and let me simply "be." Let me rest peacefully in your arms. In Christ's name I pray. Amen.

Day 8—Thursday
Didn't Anyone Else Return to Give Thanks?

Luke 17:11-19

> *Then Jesus asked, "Were not ten made clean? But the other nine, where*
> *are they? Was none of them found to return and give praise to God*
> *except this foreigner?"*
> Luke 17:17-18

At the beginning of the story in Luke 17:11-19, the Samaritan or "foreigner" has two strikes against him. He is a Samaritan, and there was at the time a long-standing rift between Samaritans and Jews. Because each considered the other ritually unclean, they avoided all contact with each other. This Samaritan is also considered unclean because he has leprosy. People with skin diseases like this were required to stay away from others at all times to avoid "contaminating" someone else. Even if a skin disease cleared up, only a priest could verify that a person was now "clean."

Luke tells us that this Samaritan and nine others with leprosy cried out for healing as Jesus came to a village. (Note that they were "keeping their distance," as required.) Jesus told all ten to go and show themselves to the priests. In the act of going, they were healed or made clean, and continued on their way. But one leper, the Samaritan, the foreigner, was different. He realized that he had been blessed, and turned back. When he returned to give thanks, Jesus said, "Get up and go on your way; your faith has made you well." The Samaritan rose and began a new way of life, a life of wholeness and gratitude.

What about the other nine who were healed? As Jesus asks not one but three questions about their whereabouts, we begin to see that he wants more than obedience from us. He wants us to give thanks and praise, to express our gratitude. He wants our hearts to overflow in thankfulness.

Biblical Wisdom
And be thankful.
Colossians 3:15b

Transformative Thought

Gratitude is not only the greatest of all virtues, but the parent of all the others.[12]
Cicero

Silence for Meditation

Psalm Fragment

O give thanks to the Lord, for he is good; his steadfast love endures forever!

Psalm 118:1

Questions to Ponder

- Name five things you thank God for today.
- How might you make gratitude to God a bigger part of your daily life? Consider using a journal to list the blessings you notice each day. If there are others in your household, you might give thanks to God together before meals or at the end of the day.

Prayer for Today

Gracious and giving God, in my busy life I sometimes forget to stop and thank you for all that you have given me. Today I thank you for (name as many things as you wish). And I thank you above all for your unconditional and eternal love. Amen.

Day 9—Friday
Do You Believe That I Am Able to Do This?

Matthew 9:27-31

As Jesus went on from there, two blind men followed him, crying loudly, "Have mercy on us, Son of David!" When he entered the house, the blind men came to him; and Jesus said to them, "Do you believe that I am able to do this?"

Matthew 9:27-28a

The two blind men in today's text had had enough of being blind! They persistently cried out, "Have mercy on us, Son of David!" as a statement of faith in God's healing power and in Jesus, the Son of David.

Jesus asked them, "Do you believe that I am able to do this?" And the men answered, "Yes, Lord." *Lord.* They confessed Jesus as Son of David and as Lord. And Jesus said, "According to your faith let it be done to you."

Have you ever heard someone say, "I'll believe it when I see it"? Seeing is believing, right? But in a profound way, the two men Jesus meets in Matthew 9 show us that *believing is seeing.* Because they believed in Jesus and his ability to heal, strengthen, and guide them, they began to see life differently. They could see how God had been active in their lives. They could look to the future with confidence in God's presence and promises.

Faith gives us a different perspective. Looking back on the past, we can see God's activity in our lives and realize that God has been with us all the time. We live in God's love and promises in the present, knowing that God is at work and with us even when we don't see it. We look to the future with the confidence that Jesus will be with us and is able to heal, strengthen, and guide us. Our eyes can't see all of this, but believing is seeing.

Biblical Wisdom
Now faith is the assurance of things hoped for, the conviction of things not seen.
Hebrews 11:1

Transformative Thought
Faith is to believe what you do not yet see; the reward for this faith is to see what you believe.[13]
St. Augustine

Silence for Meditation

Psalm Fragment

You who live in the shelter of the Most High, who abide in the shadow of the Almighty, will say to the LORD, "My refuge and my fortress; my God, in whom I trust."

Psalm 91:1-2

Questions to Ponder

- Name five things you are absolutely certain Jesus can do, and three things you sometimes wonder whether Jesus can do.
- What things do you believe in, even though you can't see them? How does faith help you see things differently?

Prayer for Today

Lord God, you have called your servants to ventures of which we cannot see the ending, by paths as yet untrodden, through perils unknown. Give us faith to go out with good courage, not knowing where we go, but only that your hand is leading us and your love supporting us; through Jesus Christ our Lord. Amen.[14]

Day 10—Saturday
Did You Not Know That I Must Be in My Father's House?

Luke 2:41-51

When his parents saw him they were astonished; and his mother said to him, "Child, why have you treated us like this? Look, your father and I have been searching for you in great anxiety." He said to them, "Why were you searching for me? Did you not know that I must be in my Father's house?"

Luke 2:48-49

It must have been a very meaningful trip to Jerusalem. Thousands of people had made their way to the temple for the Passover feast. Mary, Joseph, and Jesus were among them. Jesus was twelve years old, the age at which Jewish boys have their bar mitzvah and become a son of the Law.

But on the way home, Mary and Joseph realized that Jesus wasn't with them. When they returned to Jerusalem and found Jesus in the temple, Mary expressed her concern. Jesus responded: "Did you not know that I must be in my Father's house?"

One small word is important to notice here: *must*. "Did you not know that I *must* be in my Father's house?" *Must* reflects more than an obligation; it expresses inevitability. It expresses that something finds fullness and completion. Jesus *must* be in his Father's house.

This is the first time Jesus uses the word *must*. It appears nine other times in Luke's Gospel, and then it has to do with his preaching, teaching, suffering, and death in order to fulfill the Scriptures. *Must* reflects Jesus' priorities, dedication, and commitment to God's desires for his life, which for him took precedence over everything else.

As Luke wraps up this story of Jesus' visit to the temple, he writes, "And Jesus increased in wisdom and in years, and in divine and human favor" (Luke 2:52). Being in his Father's house was where Jesus found the real center for his life, and he was deeply committed to following God's purpose for his life.

Jesus found fullness and completion in God's house. Are you searching for something that you haven't found yet? Is your heart longing or restless? Spend time with God, spend time with the community of faith, and spend time in God's house.

Biblical Wisdom
Of course, there is great gain in godliness combined with contentment.
   1 Timothy 6:6

Transformative Thought
You have made us for yourself, O Lord, and our hearts are restless until they rest in you.[15]
   St. Augustine

Silence for Meditation

Psalm Fragment
My vows to you I must perform, O God; I will render thank offerings to you.
   Psalm 56:12

- What are some "must haves" in your life? What are some things you "must do"? What about these things makes them so important?
- Where in your life do you feel the most complete and fulfilled?

Prayer for Today

Eternal God, sustain my faith in you. Triune God, let my journey find its end in you. Giving God, let my life be enriched in you. Loving God, let me find my hope and purpose in you. In Jesus' name. Amen.

Day 11—Monday
Why Do You See the Speck in Your Neighbor's Eye?
Luke 6:39-42

> *"A disciple is not above the teacher, but everyone who is fully qualified will be like the teacher. Why do you see the speck in your neighbor's eye, but do not notice the log in your own eye?"*
> Luke 6:40-41

Jesus asks questions throughout the Gospels as a way to deepen discipleship. Rather than thinking our way into believing, Jesus asks questions to help us behave our way into believing by putting our words into action. He asks questions to invite us into a transforming relationship with him.

Jesus doesn't ask rhetorical questions, the kind that have such an obvious answer that we don't expect anyone to respond. He doesn't ask questions that can be answered simply with a "yes" or "no." Jesus doesn't do "business as usual" like this. He asks good questions, transforming questions, questions that call us to dig deep within ourselves to come up with a response.

Do I not notice the log in my own eye? Well, yes, Jesus, I do notice sometimes, but it's easier for me to see what's wrong with someone else. I try to forget about this log. It's been there so long that I don't remember how it got there, and I don't know how to get rid of it.

The season of Lent is for us often a time that is business as usual and nothing out of the ordinary. But Jesus and his questions call us to something different. We are called to let go of those things that cloud our vision and that get between us and others—and us and God. We are called to be transformed on this Lenten journey and each day of our walk with Jesus.

Biblical Wisdom
Finally, beloved, whatever is true, whatever is honorable, whatever is just, whatever is pure, whatever is pleasing, whatever is commendable, if there is any excellence and if there is anything worthy of praise, think about these things.
Philippians 4:8

Transformative Thought
When we despair of gaining inner transformation through human powers of will and determination, we are open to a wonderful new realization: inner righteousness is a gift from God to be graciously received. The needed change within us is God's work, not ours.[16]
Richard J. Foster

Silence for Meditation

Psalm Fragment
Look to him, and be radiant; so your faces shall never be ashamed.
Psalm 34:5

Questions to Ponder
· Why do you find it easier to find a speck in someone else's eye? What might be clouding your vision?
· Which of Jesus' questions has been most meaningful for you to contemplate so far? How are Jesus' questions affecting you and transforming you?

Prayer for Today
Passionate God, give me vision for what you truly want me to see. Grant me forgiveness for being quick to judge others, give me compassion for those I

encounter each day, and remove the log in my eye so I might see Jesus with fresh and clear eyes. Amen.

Day 12—Tuesday
How Much Longer Must I Put Up with You?
Matthew 17:14-21

> *Jesus answered, "You faithless and perverse generation, how much longer must I be with you? How much longer must I put up with you?"*
> Matthew 17:17

Motivational studies have shown that if you place a bunch of fleas in a shallow container, they'll quickly jump out. However, if you put a lid on the container, the fleas will jump and jump for a short time, but soon, when they sense their limits, they will quit jumping. And when you remove the lid, they'll remain in the container instead of jumping out, because they've been programmed to know the limits of what they can do.

In the same way, a circus elephant is trained as a baby to stay put. Tied to a heavy stake secured in the ground, a young elephant quickly learns that a tug on the leg means it can't go anywhere. By the time the elephant is full-grown, it quits pulling as soon as it feels a tug on the leg, because it has learned there's no use trying to get away.

In Matthew 17:14-21 Jesus seems angry. And he is—not because of something the disciples are doing, but because of what they aren't doing. They had tried to heal a man with epilepsy, but with no results. So the man's family brings him to Jesus. Comparing the disciples to a faithless and perverse generation, Jesus laments about how much longer he will be with them. They are not doing what they could be doing, what Jesus has called and empowered them to do.

Maybe the disciples had been programmed for mediocrity, like those fleas that quit jumping or the elephant that quit pulling. Whatever the reason for their behavior, shortly after Jesus' lament, he says, "For truly I tell you, if you have faith the size of a mustard seed, you will say to this mountain, 'Move from here to there,' and it will move; and nothing will be impossible for you" (Matthew 17:20b).

You may have been programmed for mediocrity at some time in your life, but that is not who you are. You are a child of God. Jesus calls you to follow him and serve others and God. The Holy Spirit empowers you with faith, and even faith the size of a mustard seed, one of the tiniest of seeds, can do great things. Your life of faith is one of immense potential, surprising possibilities, and amazing promise.

Biblical Wisdom
Jesus looked at them and said, "For mortals it is impossible, but not for God; for God all things are possible."
   Mark 10:27

Transformative Thought
I am only one, but still I am one. I cannot do everything, but still I can do something; and because I cannot do everything, I will not refuse to do something that I can do.[17]
   Edward Everett Hale

Silence for Meditation

Psalm Fragment
This is my comfort in my distress, that your promise gives me life.
   Psalm 119:50

Questions to Ponder
- Reflect on a time you accomplished something that you weren't sure you could do. How did that feel?
- During this Lenten journey, what might God be calling and empowering you to do?

Prayer for Today
Mighty and powerful God, forgive me for the times I haven't done what you have called and empowered me to do. Strengthen my faith and increase my love for you and others. Guide me to live out my calling each day. In Jesus' name. Amen.

Week Three
Who Do You Say That I Am?

Day 13—Wednesday
But Who Do You Say That I Am?
Mark 8:27-30

> *Jesus went on with his disciples to the villages of Caesarea Philippi; and*
> *on the way he asked his disciples, "Who do people say that I am?" And*
> *they answered him, "John the Baptist; and others, Elijah; and still others,*
> *one of the prophets." He asked them, "But who do you say that I am?"*
> Mark 8:27-29a

Certainly people living in his time wondered who Jesus was and what he could do. The disciples tell Jesus that some people see him as another John the Baptist, or maybe the great prophet Elijah come back to life. Others think he might be another in a long line of prophets. Then Jesus gets down to business by asking a serious, probing, and transformative question: Who do *you* say that I am?"

It's easy to talk about what other people think or believe. We don't have any stake in that. In the world today we can find people with all kinds of views about who Jesus is or isn't. But who do *you* say Jesus is? This isn't just a question for the disciples. It's a question for you and for me, and for the community of faith.

Jesus uses questions as a way to deepen discipleship and grow faith. The question "Who do you say I am?" is an invitation into deeper relationship with Jesus and with others. Transforming the way we see Jesus, ourselves, and the world transforms our lives.

Biblical Wisdom
If you confess with your lips that Jesus is Lord and believe in your heart
that God raised him from the dead, you will be saved.
Romans 10:9

Transformative Thought
What, then, does Jesus mean to me? To me, he was one of the greatest teachers humanity has ever had. To his believers, he was God's only begotten Son.[18]
Mahatma Gandhi

Silence for Meditation

Psalm Fragment
I call upon the LORD, who is worthy to be praised, so I shall be saved from my enemies.
    Psalm 18:3

Questions to Ponder
- What major misconceptions about Jesus have you heard?
- Think about how you would describe Jesus to a friend who has had no connections with the Bible or the church. Who would you say Jesus is?

Prayer for Today
Jesus, you are God with us and Son of God. You are my Savior and the Savior of the world. You are my Lord and the eternal Lord of all creation. Keep me always close to you. In your holy name I pray. Amen.

Day 14—Thursday
Do You Not Believe That I Am in the Father and the Father Is in Me?
    John 14:8-14

Philip said to him, "Lord, show us the Father, and we will be satisfied." Jesus said to him, "Have I been with you all this time, Philip, and you still do not know me? Whoever has seen me has seen the Father. How can you say, 'Show us the Father'? Do you not believe that I am in the Father and the Father is in me?"
    John 14:8-10a

I love Burger King. I love to "have it my way" when I order a hamburger. I order it with extra catsup and sometimes onions. I love having so many options available to me.

But we are not Burger King Christians. You can't have Jesus the way you want him. *Yes, I'll take the Jesus Burger, but hold off on the challenging stuff in the Sermon on the Mount, or that thing about taking up my cross. I'd like Jesus my way.*

Like it or not, we can't have Jesus our way. There's just no getting around the fact that God is God. It's that plain and simple: God is God, and we are not God. And Jesus is in God. He is God with us. No matter how much we might like it to be different, when we say Jesus is Lord, he is in the lead and we are followers. When we say Jesus is Savior, it means he saves us from sin and death. We don't save ourselves. God is God, and we are not God.

So what does this mean for us on our journey through Lent? It means we acknowledge and praise who God is and who Jesus is. It means that instead of trying to have everything our way, we follow the way of Jesus.

Biblical Wisdom
I pray that the God of our Lord Jesus Christ, the Father of glory, may give you a spirit of wisdom and revelation as you come to know him, so that, with the eyes of your heart enlightened, you may know what is the hope to which he has called you, what are the riches of his glorious inheritance among the saints, and what is the immeasurable greatness of his power for us who believe, according to the working of his great power.
Ephesians 1:17-19

Transformative Thought
Let us ever walk with Jesus, follow his example pure,
through a world that would deceive us and to sin our spirits lure.
Onward in his footsteps treading, trav'lers here, our home above,
full of faith and hope and love, let us do our Savior's bidding.
Faithful Lord, with me abide; I shall follow where you guide.[19]
Sigismund von Birken

Silence for Meditation

Psalm Fragment

When I look at your heavens, the work of your fingers, the moon and the
stars that you have established; what are human beings that you are
mindful of them, mortals that you care for them?
  Psalm 8:3-4

Questions to Ponder

- What do you think about being a Burger King Christian? Does it bother you
  that you can't have God or Jesus your own way?
- What might need to happen for you to follow Jesus more closely and not
  simply go your own way?

Prayer for Today

Dear Jesus, God with us, turn my heart to you. Turn my life to you. Guide me on
your path. In your holy name I pray. Amen.

Day 15—Friday
Did I Not Tell You That You Would See the Glory of God?
  John 11:38-44

Then Jesus, again greatly disturbed, came to the tomb. It was a cave,
and a stone was lying against it. Jesus said, "Take away the stone."
Martha, the sister of the dead man, said to him, "Lord, already there is a
stench because he has been dead four days." Jesus said to her, "Did I not
tell you that if you believed, you would see the glory of God?"
  John 11:38-40

Someone told Jesus that his friend Lazarus was very ill, and what did he do? He
stayed where he was for two more days. He said he would be glorified through
Lazarus's illness (John 11:4), so he waited. Now, I'm a very patient person, as long
as things happen right away! In times of illness and death, it's especially difficult
to wait. It's difficult to see anything beyond the immediate crisis.

When Jesus finally arrived, Lazarus had been in the tomb for four days.
There was a common belief in Jesus' time that a person's spirit stayed with them

for three days after they died but left on the fourth day. So after four days in the tomb, there was no doubt that Lazarus really was dead. And as Martha said, there was a stench! Lazarus was dead, and his body was beginning to smell.

Jesus knew what God was doing, so he waited to come. Death would not be the end of the story here. The story of Lazarus would become a testament to God's glory. Mary and Martha were overjoyed when their brother Lazarus was raised. At the end of the waiting, God was glorified.

At the end of his musical compositions, Johann Sebastian Bach would write the letters S.D.G., shorthand for *Soli Deo Gloria*, a Latin phrase meaning "glory to God alone." Difficult times in life are not the end of our story. Death is not the end of our story. God will be glorified. Glory to God alone!

Biblical Wisdom
And the Word became flesh and lived among us, and we have seen his glory, the glory as of a father's only son, full of grace and truth.
    John 1:14

Transformative Thought
I would rather live in a world where my life is surrounded by mystery than live in a world so small that my mind could comprehend it.[20]
Harry Emerson Fosdick

Silence for Meditation

Psalm Fragment
I waited patiently for the Lord; he inclined to me and heard my cry.
    Psalm 40:1

Questions to Ponder
- When have you waited for God to answer a prayer, or had God answer a prayer in an unexpected way? What was the outcome?
- Remember a time when you received a glimpse of God's glory. (Maybe this happened as you and another person forgave one another and were reconciled, as you sang or heard the soaring lyrics and music of a song, or as you

received the bread and wine of Holy Communion.) How would you describe this experience? Now imagine the glory of God that still awaits you.

Prayer for Today

I waited for the Lord, he inclined unto me, he heard my complaint. O blest are they that hope and trust in him.[21] In Jesus' name. Amen.

Day 16—Saturday
Are You a Teacher of Israel, and Yet You Do Not Understand These Things?

John 3:1-21

> *Nicodemus said to him, "How can these things be?" Jesus answered him, "Are you a teacher of Israel, and yet you do not understand these things?"*
> John 3:9-10

There was no doubt that Nicodemus had done very well on the ladder of success. He was a Pharisee, which meant he spent hours and hours reading the Torah, or law, memorizing and researching and thinking about how to be a devout follower of God. He observed every detail of the law every moment of his life. He was a leader of the Jews, revered and held in high esteem by many people around him.

Nicodemus dropped by one night, looking for Jesus. And when Jesus started talking about a new birth by water and the Spirit, he was confused. How could this be?

To illustrate what he was saying, Jesus referred to a story from Scripture. During the ancient Israelites' journey through the wilderness, after God freed them from slavery in Egypt, many people were bitten by poisonous snakes and died. God told Moses, their leader, to make a bronze serpent and put it on a pole. Those who were bitten by the snakes and looked at the serpent on the pole did not die (Numbers 21:4-9). So Jesus said, "Just as Moses lifted up the serpent in the wilderness, so must the Son of Man be lifted up, that whoever believes in him may have eternal life. For God so loved the world that he gave his only Son, that everyone who believes in him may not perish but have eternal life" (John 3:14-16).

Nicodemus knew a lot *about* God, but now he was invited to know the one who *is* God, who came down from heaven to give his life for us and the world. In the way we looked at life on Day 3 (pages 25–27), we could say this successful man was invited into a life of significance. How did Nicodemus respond to this invitation? What happened to him after this talk with Jesus?

Nicodemus is mentioned only in John's Gospel and just two more times after this (7:45-52; 19:38-42). In the midst of an argument among the temple police, chief priests, and Pharisees about what should be done with Jesus, Nicodemus points out that the law does not allow a judgment without a hearing. Then he doesn't appear again until after Jesus dies on the cross. He and Joseph of Arimathea take Jesus' body, wrap it with cloths and spices according to Jewish customs at that time, and lay it in a tomb.

Biblical Wisdom

More than that, I regard everything as loss because of the surpassing value of knowing Christ Jesus my Lord. For his sake I have suffered the loss of all things, and I regard them as rubbish, in order that I may gain Christ.

Philippians 3:8

Transformative Thought

What then remains but that we still should cry
Not to be born, or, being born, to die?[22]
Francis Bacon

Silence for Meditation

Psalm Fragment

Praise him for his mighty deeds; praise him according to his surpassing greatness!

Psalm 150:2

- What do you think happened to Nicodemus? How would you fill in the blanks in his story?
- During this Lenten season, how will you keep your eyes on Jesus? How will you respond to his invitation to know him more deeply?

Prayer for Today

Gracious and loving God, help me to move more deeply from knowing about you to knowing and loving you, from seeking success to living with significance, from keeping faith to myself to sharing your story with others. Strengthen and empower me to look to Jesus for life now and forever. Amen.

17—Monday
Why Do You Not Do What I Tell You?
Luke 6:46-49

"Why do you call me 'Lord, Lord,' and do not do what I tell you? I will show you what someone is like who comes to me, hears my words, and acts on them."
Luke 6:46-47

Jesus' questions seem too probing, too intense, and there are just so many of them. Isn't it enough that the disciples call him Lord? Are they really also supposed to do everything he tells them to? Isn't it enough to say we're Christians? Are we really supposed to follow Jesus too? That might be going a bit too far!

Keep in mind that Jesus uses questions as a way to deepen our lives of discipleship. Jesus explains today's question in this way: Someone who hears his words and acts on them is like a wise man who builds his house on a foundation of solid rock, but a person who hears Jesus' words and doesn't act on them is like a foolish man who builds a house with no foundation.

This connection between what we hear and what we do doesn't come naturally and goes against many of society's expectations. It goes against putting ourselves first and doing whatever we need to do to get ahead. It goes against telling "white lies" rather than speaking the truth. It goes against saying one thing and doing another.

Yet it is clear that Jesus looks for us to not only say he is Lord, but to do what he says. He seeks consistency between our beliefs and our behavior, our convictions and our conduct, our values and our lifestyle. He calls us to live with *integrity*, a word that comes from the root "to integrate." Integrity means integrating our beliefs and daily behavior. This isn't something you just slip into. Living with integrity is a decision. It's a daily commitment. Saying Jesus is Lord and doing what he says means aligning our convictions with our conduct, what we believe with how we act, every day. Now that's a solid foundation!

Biblical Wisdom
The righteous walk in integrity—happy are the children who follow them!
Proverbs 20:7

Transformative Thought
Our secular lives need the vision, reverence, piety, values, reflection, service, and commitments offered by a spiritual sensibility.[23]
Thomas Moore

Silence for Meditation

Psalm Fragment
But as for me, I walk in my integrity; redeem me, and be gracious to me.
Psalm 26:11

Questions to Ponder
- What does it really mean to call Jesus your Lord?
- Think about someone you know who lives with great integrity. What could you learn from this person's example?

Prayer for Today

Lord of all creation, you are Lord of my life too. Help me to hear and do what you say. Give me the courage and strength to match my words and my actions. Keep me close as I follow you. This I pray in Jesus' name. Amen.

Day 18—Tuesday
Will You Lay Down Your Life for Me?
John 13:36-38

> *Peter said to him, "Lord, why can I not follow you now? I will lay down my life for you." Jesus answered, "Will you lay down your life for me?"*
> John 13:37-38a

Several years ago a young girl at Stanford Medical Hospital was diagnosed with a rare and very serious disease. Doctors determined that the only option was to give the girl a complete blood transfusion from her five-year-old brother. In surviving the same disease, he had developed antibodies to fight it. The doctors knew that, at his age, the boy couldn't understand everything that was going on, so they just asked him if he would be willing to help out his big sister by giving her his blood. The boy looked at the doctors, looked at his sister, and agreed to help.

As the little boy lay in the bed next to his sister and saw his blood starting to pass from his arm to hers, he looked up at the doctor and said with a trembling voice, "Will I start to die right away, or will it take a while?" At that moment the doctor realized the boy believed he was giving up his life for his sister.[24]

Would you be willing to give up your life for someone or something? This is not an easy question. Are you willing to lay down your life for Jesus? This is the haunting question Peter was asked. It's a question that shakes us to the core if we take it seriously. Surely there must be another way. This time Jesus is asking for too much. Who does he think he is?

Are you willing to lay down your life for me? The one who asks you this question has already laid down his life for you.

Biblical Wisdom
No one has greater love than this, to lay down one's life for one's friends.
   John 15:13

Transformative Thought
A man who won't die for something is not fit to live.[25]
Martin Luther King Jr.

Silence for Meditation

Psalm Fragment
The sacrifice acceptable to God is a broken spirit; a broken and contrite heart, O God, you will not despise.
   Psalm 51:17

Questions to Ponder
- How would you describe the little boy who thought he was giving up his life for his sister?
- Jesus gave up his life for you. What thoughts and feelings do you have about this? How do you react to his question about giving up your life for him?

Prayer for Today
Lord Jesus, I am in awe that you gave up your life for me. Teach me and guide me to give my life over to you, day after day. In your holy name I pray. Amen.

Week Four
What Do You Want Me to Do for You?

Day 19—Wednesday
What Do You Want Me to Do for You?
Matthew 20:29-34

> *There were two blind men sitting by the roadside. When they heard that*
> *Jesus was passing by, they shouted, "Lord, have mercy on us, Son of*
> *David!" The crowd sternly ordered them to be quiet; but they shouted*
> *even more loudly, "Have mercy on us, Lord, Son of David!" Jesus stood*
> *still and called them, saying, "What do you want me to do for you?"*
> Matthew 20:30-32

Jesus is always on the move in the Gospels, so it isn't surprising in this Scripture reading to find him going from one place to another. On this day, two men shout out to him from the side of the road. The people in the crowd try to keep the men quiet. (Maybe they want to prevent a disturbance, or just make sure they can hear anything Jesus might say. Maybe they think Jesus is too busy or too important to stop for these two people.) But the men call out even louder to Jesus.

Instead of continuing on, staying on schedule, and doing what's expected of him, Jesus stops, stands still, and asks the men a question. He focuses on what they need and what only he can give. They say, "Lord, let our eyes be opened." Out of compassion, Jesus touches their eyes. And with their sight restored, they follow him.

We might expect Jesus, as Lord of all, to ask people, "What can you do for *me?*" but that never happens. In fact, in the Gospels Jesus asks "What do you want me to do for *you?*" more often than any other question. And he doesn't just ask—he listens for the response. The response from the two men shows who they believe Jesus is and what they believe Jesus can do. They believe Jesus is Lord and that he can make them see again, and they immediately follow him.

Who do you believe Jesus is? What do you believe he can do? What do you want him to do for you?

Biblical Wisdom

But Jesus looked at them and said, "For mortals it is impossible, but for God all things are possible."
  Matthew 19:26

Transformative Thought

You see things; and you say, "Why?" But I dream things that never were; and I say, "Why not?"[26]
George Bernard Shaw

Silence for Meditation

Psalm Fragment

The Lord opens the eyes of the blind. The Lord lifts up those who are bowed down; the Lord loves the righteous.
  Psalm 146:8

Questions to Ponder

- In your life, where or when do you need to "stand still"? How can you begin to do that?
- What needs do you believe Jesus can meet? What do you want Jesus to do for you?

Prayer for Today

Loving Jesus, help me to see you, trust you, worship you, and follow you. Amen.

Day 20—Thursday
Did You Lack Anything?
  Luke 9:1-6; 22:35-36

He said to them, "When I sent you out without a purse, bag, or sandals, did you lack anything?"
  Luke 22:35a

Today's question from Jesus comes at an ominous point in Luke's Gospel. Jesus and the disciples have celebrated the Passover meal, which remembers how God freed the ancient Israelites from slavery in Egypt. At this meal Jesus passed around a loaf of bread and a cup of wine, saying they were his body and blood, and to share them in remembrance of him. He told the disciples that one of them would betray him and that Peter would deny him three times before the cock crowed again.

As Jesus and the disciples are about to face his arrest, trial, and crucifixion, he now refers back to an earlier time. In effect he says, "Remember the time when I sent you out on that mission trip without any provisions—no bag, food, money, or change of clothes? How did that work out?" We don't need to hear the disciples' answer, because Luke has already reported on the trip's success. The disciples "went through the villages, bringing the good news and curing diseases everywhere" (9:6). God provided for the disciples when they took nothing with them. They shared the good news and healed people.

Today—and every day—Jesus calls us to remember. Remember, God knit you together in your mother's womb, and you are fearfully and wonderfully made (Psalm 139). Remember, God has always been faithful to God's people. Remember, God will provide for you. Remember, God empowers you to bring good news and healing to others. Remember, share Christ's body and blood with one another.

Remember who you are. Remember what God has done for you.

Biblical Wisdom
But he said to me, "My grace is sufficient for you, for power is made perfect in weakness." So, I will boast all the more gladly of my weaknesses, so that the power of Christ may dwell in me.
   2 Corinthians 12:9

Transformative Thought
Stories have to be told or they die, and when they die, we can't remember who we are or why we're here.[27]
   Sue Monk Kidd

Silence for Meditation

Psalm Fragment

Come and see what God has done: he is awesome in his deeds among mortals. He turned the sea into dry land; they passed through the river on foot. There we rejoiced in him.
   Psalm 66:5-6

Questions to Ponder

· What times in the past does your family or congregation take time to remember? What is important about sharing stories like those?
· What past experiences are important for you to remember as you walk with Jesus? How does remembering these events help you here and now?

Prayer for Today

Gracious God, you give me far more than I can ask for or imagine on this journey through life. When I face difficult times, help me remember that I am your child and you are faithful. You have pulled me through before, and you will pull me through again. In Jesus' name. Amen.

Day 21—Friday
Which Is Easier, Declaring Forgiveness or Healing?
   Luke 5:17-26

> *Then the scribes and the Pharisees began to question, "Who is this who is speaking blasphemies? Who can forgive sins but God alone?" When Jesus perceived their questionings, he answered them, "Why do you raise such questions in your hearts? Which is easier, to say, 'Your sins are forgiven you,' or to say, 'Stand up and walk'?"*
> Luke 5:21-23

As the story in Luke 5:17-26 begins, Jesus has healed many of diseases, and people are eager to hear what he has to say and see what he does. On this day, a crowd has gathered at a house, and a group of Pharisees and scribes, teachers of the law, is seated nearby. Some men arrive with a friend who has a form of paralysis. They carry this man on his bed and unsuccessfully try to squeeze their way through the crowd to get to Jesus inside. But they don't give up. They climb up on the roof, remove some tiles, and lower the man and his bed right down in front of Jesus.

In the middle of this major disruption, Jesus notices the men's faith and tells their friend that his sins are forgiven. The teachers, well-acquainted with the law, start to raise questions. They say that by daring to speak for God, the only one who can forgive sins, Jesus has committed blasphemy.

Aware of this controversy, Jesus asks, "Which is easier, to say, 'Your sins are forgiven you,' or to say, 'Stand up and walk'?" And then, to show his authority on earth to forgive sins, Jesus tells the man who is paralyzed to get up and walk. The man stands up, picks up his bed, heads home, and gives glory to God. Everyone else is filled with awe and amazement and glorifies God too.

This is a story filled with interesting characters and dramatic action. Jesus speaks and acts with authority and shows his power to forgive and to heal. What questions would we have had for him? How far will we go to bring someone to Jesus? How will we give thanks and praise for all God has done for us and those around us?

Biblical Wisdom

In him we have redemption through his blood, the forgiveness of our trespasses, according to the riches of his grace.
Ephesians 1:7

Transformative Thought

The weak can never forgive. Forgiveness is the attribute of the strong.[28]
Mahatma Gandhi

Silence for Meditation

Psalm Fragment

For his anger is but for a moment; his favor is for a lifetime. Weeping may linger for the night, but joy comes with the morning.
Psalm 30:5

Questions to Ponder

- Which of the characters in this story is most like you—Jesus, someone in the crowd, a teacher of the law, one of those bringing a friend to Jesus, or the person who was healed? Why?
- In what ways do you need forgiveness or healing (or both) from Jesus today? How will you glorify God for these gifts? How will you bring forgiveness or healing to the lives of others?

Prayer for Today

Lord Jesus, you have the power to forgive, and I ask your forgiveness for the hurtful things I've done and the things I should have done. Give me the grace to let go of resentment and the strength to forgive others. You have the power to heal, and I ask for healing of my body, mind, and spirit. Give me the perseverance to bring others to you, in spite of the obstacles. To the glory of your name. Amen.

Day 22—Saturday
Who Are My Mother and My Brothers?
Mark 3:31-35

> *A crowd was sitting around him; and they said to him, "Your mother and your brothers and sisters are outside, asking for you." And he replied, "Who are my mother and my brothers?"*
> Mark 3:32-33

Many years ago I attended an adult immersion baptism at Holden Village, a Lutheran retreat center in the North Cascades, where people gather every week for fellowship, hiking, study, worship, and personal growth.

Rick, a young adult with a difficult background, came to know Jesus and wanted to be baptized in Railroad Creek, a glacier-fed stream running through Holden Village. After the worship service one evening, we went to the creek, where Rick was standing waist-deep in the water with Holden's pastor.

When the pastor said, "I baptize you in the name of the Father!" he put his hand on Rick's head and pushed him beneath the icy waters. The rest of us got chills just watching. Rick came up for air, and all of a sudden the pastor said,

"And of the Son!" Rick took a big breath just before the pastor pushed him back under the water. After what seemed too long a time, the pastor let Rick come up for another gasp of air then said, "And of the Holy Spirit!" and plunged Rick under water for a third time. Now the rest of us were starting to shake, we were so cold watching what was happening.

Afterward I asked Rick, "So what was it like, getting baptized and all?" He said, "Man, it was terrible. I thought I was going to die." I thought to myself, "Bingo!" That's it. Baptism is dying to the life that we had before knowing Jesus. Baptism gives a new direction to our lives. Baptism puts to death that old life and gives birth to a new one. We die to the old and rise to the new. Now we are part of God's family, brothers and sisters in Christ, called to love one another and serve our neighbors.

Biblical Wisdom
So if anyone is in Christ, there is a new creation: everything old has passed away; see, everything has become new!
  2 Corinthians 5:17

Transformative Thought
Every ending is a new beginning. Through the grace of God, we can always start again.[29]
  Marianne Williamson

Silence for Meditation

Psalm Fragment
O sing to the LORD a new song; sing to the LORD, all the earth.
  Psalm 96:1

Questions to Ponder
- Think about your own baptism or one you have witnessed. Who was there? Did anything unusual or unexpected happen?
- In your congregation, how might love for one another and service to others be deepened?

Prayer for Today

Gracious God, blest be the tie that binds our hearts in Christian love, the unity of heart and mind is like to that above.[30] In the name of Jesus, our brother. Amen.

Day 23—Monday
Can Saltiness Be Restored?
Matthew 5:13-16

> *"You are the salt of the earth; but if salt has lost its taste, how can its saltiness be restored?"*
> Matthew 5:13a

Salt is indispensable in our lives. It's essential for all the life that flourishes in oceans and saltwater seas. It has been used for several thousand years to preserve food and keep it from spoiling. Our bodies can't function without it. Before we are born, we grow and develop in a salt solution. Without salt our hearts would not beat, our blood would not flow, and our muscles would not work properly. Blood, sweat, and tears all contain salt.

In biblical times, salt was so precious that it may have been used to pay Roman soldiers. The word *salary*, in fact, comes from the Latin word for "salt." Maybe that is why we say people who deserve to be rewarded or paid are "worth their salt."

Jesus compares us to this indispensable, life-sustaining, precious substance when he says, "You are the salt of the earth." He also says, "You are the light of the world" (Matthew 5:14a). Those are declarative statements: you *are* salt, you *are* light. Jesus doesn't say, "If you wouldn't mind, when you have some spare time, could you be salt? Could you be a moral and faithful preservative in a world showing signs of decay?" You don't get to vote on this either. As a follower of Jesus, you are salt and you are light.

Following Jesus means being salt and light in the midst of the decay brought about by greed, corporate scandals, violence, homelessness, poverty, and more. The salt and light you bring may not seem like much to you, but they make a difference to the people you encounter from day to day.

There is no hope of restoration for salt that loses its taste, but there is always hope for us. Our "saltiness" is renewed, refreshed, and restored as we gather with other "salty" characters in the family of God, as we ask for and receive forgiveness, and as Christ makes us new each day.

We are the salt of the earth. We are the light of the world.

Biblical Wisdom

Clothe yourselves with the new self, created according to the likeness of God in true righteousness and holiness.

Ephesians 4:24

Transformative Thought

But these few are the salt of the earth; without them, human life would become a stagnant pool. Not only is it they who introduce good things which did not before exist, it is they who keep the life in those which already existed.[31]

John Stuart Mill

Silence for Meditation

Psalm Fragment

Preserve my life, for I am devoted to you; save your servant who trusts in you. You are my God.

Psalm 86:2

Questions to Ponder

- Name some people who are "salt of the earth" in your life or in your community. How do they maintain their saltiness?
- What can you do to bring salt or light into a place that needs it?

Prayer for Today

Dear God, guide me and teach me to be salt and light in the world. When I am running on empty and feel I have nothing left to give, restore me and fill me again. Let my light shine and bring glory to you. In Jesus' precious and holy name. Amen.

Day 24—Tuesday
What Is the Kingdom of God Like?
Luke 13:18-21

[Jesus] said therefore, "What is the kingdom of God like?"
Luke 13:18a

Jesus wanted to explain something about the kingdom of God to his followers, so he compared it to two small, familiar things: a mustard seed and baking yeast. A tiny mustard seed grows into a bush or tree large enough to hold birds and their nests, he said, while a small amount of yeast leavens and transforms an entire loaf of bread. The kingdom of God, it seems, doesn't stay the same. It might start small, but it grows and changes in surprising ways.

Disciples or followers of Jesus don't stay the same either. As we walk with Jesus, we grow and change. The apostle Paul described this transformation: "Do not be conformed to this world, but be transformed by the renewing of your minds, so that you may discern what is the will of God—what is good and acceptable and perfect" (Romans 12:2). But how does renewal of our minds happen?

I like to think of this renewal as reorienting the "autopilot" of our lives to other coordinates. By autopilot I mean the way we automatically think and act. If we want to change things in our lives, but our autopilot settings stay the same, we go right back to falling into the same traps and doing the same things. So to identify your autopilot settings, complete the following sentences.

With my time, it's just like me to be . . .

With my family, it's just like me to be . . .

With my money, it's just like me to be . . .

Whatever you discover here, by Jesus' power and through the Holy Spirit, you can be renewed and transformed. If it's just like you to focus on success, you can be transformed to focus on significance. If it's just like you to focus on yourself, you can be transformed to focus on others. If it's just like you to focus on what you can get, you can be transformed to focus on giving and generosity.

During this Lenten journey, let the questions of Jesus and the time you spend in reflection and prayer be seeds and leaven for change and growth in faith. As you walk with Jesus, you are on a journey of transformation throughout your life.

Biblical Wisdom
And all of us . . . are being transformed into the same image from one degree of glory to another; for this comes from the Lord, the Spirit.
    2 Corinthians 3:18

Transformative Thought
We need to be the change we wish to see in the world.[32]
Mahatma Gandhi

Silence for Meditation

Psalm Fragment
The Lord is my strength and my shield; in him my heart trusts; so I am helped, and my heart exults, and with my song I give thanks to him.
    Psalm 28:7

Questions to Ponder
- What would you say the kingdom of God is like?
- Reflect on your life to this point, your walk with Jesus, and any times when you have been changed or transformed. Then consider how God might be changing or transforming you now.

Prayer for Today
Transforming God, take my life, my will, my intellect, and my heart and make them truly yours. Guide me, lead me, walk beside me, and transform me. In Jesus' holy name. Amen.

Week Five
Do You Love Me?

Day 25—Wednesday
Do You Love [*Agape*] Me?

John 21:1-16

> *When they had finished breakfast, Jesus said to Simon Peter, "Simon son of John, do you love [agape] me more than these?" He said to him, "Yes, Lord; you know that I love [phileo] you." Jesus said to him, "Feed my lambs." A second time he said to him, "Simon son of John, do you love [agape] me?" He said to him, "Yes, Lord; you know that I love [phileo] you."*
>
> John 21:15-16a

Do you love Jesus?

It's an important question. In fact, it's a fundamental, transformative question. Do you love Jesus?

Today's Scripture reading is from John 21, the last chapter in John's Gospel. Jesus appears to his disciples after he has been raised from the dead, and he asks Peter, "Simon, son of John, do you love me?" He asks a second time. And a third time.

Tomorrow we'll take a closer look at these three questions from Jesus and at *agape* and *phileo*, Greek words that mean two very different types of love. Today let's take a closer look at Peter.

In many ways we might say that Peter is the premier disciple. Whenever the disciples are named in the Gospels, Simon Peter is first on the list. He has the courage to get out of a boat and walk on water toward Jesus. Jesus renames him Cephas, the "rock," and says he will build his church on Peter's declaration that Jesus is the Messiah, the Son of God. Peter is always there by Jesus' side.

But there are many "lows" in Peter's life too. On the stormy seas, when Peter takes his eyes off Jesus, he begins to sink into the turbulent water. When he hears that Jesus will suffer, he says, "God forbid, no!" When Jesus is on trial, he denies even knowing Jesus—not once, but three times.

Maybe that's why Jesus asks Peter three times, "Do you love me?" Jesus gives Peter not one, not two, but three opportunities to redeem himself after denying Jesus three times.

Do you love Jesus? Even if you've had lows in your life when you've taken your eyes off Jesus, you can still say yes. Even if you've had lows in your life when you've flat-out denied Jesus, you can still say yes. God, after all, is a God of second chances, and third. . . .

Biblical Wisdom

Beloved, let us love one another, because love is from God; everyone who loves is born of God and knows God.
    1 John 4:7

Transformative Thought

Love is a mighty power, a great and complete good; Love alone lightens every burden, and makes the rough places smooth. It bears every hardship as though it were nothing, and renders all bitterness sweet and acceptable. The love of Jesus is noble, and inspires us to great deeds; it moves us always to desire perfection.[33]
    Thomas à Kempis

Silence for Meditation

Psalm Fragment

We ponder your steadfast love, O God, in the midst of your temple.
    Psalm 48:9

Questions to Ponder

- What helps you to keep your eyes on Jesus?
- In your opinion, why did Jesus give Peter a second and third chance? When have you been given a second chance, and what did you do with it?

Prayer for Today

O God, you have prepared for those who love you joys beyond understanding. Pour into our hearts such love for you that, loving you above all things, we may obtain your promises, which exceed all that we can desire; through Jesus Christ, your Son and our Lord, who lives and reigns with you and the Holy Spirit, one God, now and forever. Amen.[34]

Day 26—Thursday
Do You Love [*Phileo*] Me?
John 21:16-19

> *He said to him the third time, "Simon son of John, do you love [phileo]*
> *me?" Peter felt hurt because he said to him the third time, "Do you love*
> *[phileo] me?" And he said to him, "Lord, you know everything; you know*
> *that I love [phileo] you."*
> John 21:17

Do you love Jesus?

In the Greek language there is more than one word to describe love. The first and most important word for love is *agape*. Agape is the deepest form of love, based on sacrificial living for another. Agape is loving with all your heart, soul, mind, and strength. Another Greek word to describe love is *phileo*. Phileo is brotherly or sisterly love for another. (The Greek words *phileo* and *adelphos*, "brother," combine to form "Philadelphia," known as the "city of brotherly love.")

These two forms of love come into play in the questions Jesus asks and in Peter's responses. The first two times Jesus asks Peter, "Do you love me?" *agape* is the kind of love Jesus refers to. Jesus is looking for a sacrificial love, the kind of love that gives all, just as Jesus gave his life for the sake of those who follow him. Twice Peter answers, "Yes, Lord, I love you," referring to the *phileo* form of love. Peter isn't able to respond with the sacrificial love Jesus is looking for. He responds, "I love you, Jesus." Yeah, we're tight, man. You're just like a brother to me.

So, the third time, Jesus changes the question, "Peter, do you love me?," this time using the *phileo* form of love. And Peter says, "Lord, you know everything; you know that I love [*phileo*] you."

Knowing that Peter is not capable of *agape* love, Jesus asks the third question on Peter's level. Jesus loves Peter just the way he is, with all his quirks and idiosyncrasies, with all his enthusiasm and all his failures. Jesus loves him unconditionally, without reserve. But Jesus changes the question to address Peter's level of love. At the same time, Jesus loves Peter far too much to let him stay that way.

He wants Peter to grow to love him with an *agape* form of love that gives heart, soul, mind, and strength.

In the same way, Jesus loves us unconditionally, without reserve, with a love that never ends. He loves us and accepts us just as we are. And he loves us far too much to let us stay as we are. He wants us to grow to really love him as he loves us—with *agape* love that doesn't hold back anything.

Do you love Jesus?

Biblical Wisdom
I am confident of this, that the one who began a good work among you
will bring it to completion by the day of Jesus Christ.
Philippians 1:6

Transformative Thought
It is unearned love—the love that goes before, that greets us on the way. It's the help you receive when you have no bright ideas left, when you are empty and desperate and have discovered that your best thinking and most charming charm have failed you. Grace is the light or electricity or juice or breeze that takes you from that isolated place and puts you with others who are as startled and embarrassed and eventually grateful as you are to be there.[35]
Anne Lamott

Silence for Meditation

Psalm Fragment
For your steadfast love is before my eyes, and I walk in faithfulness to you.
Psalm 26:3

Questions to Ponder
- When and where have you been most aware that Jesus loves you? What words, songs, or images does Jesus' love bring to mind for you?
- Worshiping, praying, giving, reading the Bible, teaching, inviting, and serving are among the many ways we can grow and develop in our love for Jesus

and for others. Consider making one of these practices a more regular part of your life in the remaining days in Lent.

Prayer for Today

Jesus loves me! this I know, for the Bible tells me so; little ones to him belong, they are weak, but he is strong. Yes, Jesus loves me, yes, Jesus loves me, yes, Jesus loves me, the Bible tells me so.[36] Amen.

Day 27—Friday
Which of You Does Not Seek the Lost One?
Luke 15:3-7

> *"Which one of you, having a hundred sheep and losing one of them, does not leave the ninety-nine in the wilderness and go after the one that is lost until he finds it?"*
> Luke 15:4

What if your congregation became known as a place that welcomes the lost, or as a place where the lost are found?

Luke 15 is fondly referred to as the "lost" chapter. It includes three stories from Jesus, about a lost sheep, a lost coin, and lost brothers. What's fascinating is that in each of the stories, when the lost are found there's a huge celebration! People call together their friends and neighbors, and say, "Rejoice with me, for I have found [what] I had lost." And Jesus says, "Just so, I tell you, there will be more joy in heaven over one sinner who repents than over ninety-nine righteous persons who need no repentance" (15:7).

Would any of us leave ninety-nine sheep on their own in the wild to chase after one that strayed from the flock? People in Jesus' time would have laughed at this question. Unattended sheep could easily scatter and fall prey to wild animals. But unlike us, the shepherd is willing to risk everything to find one lost sheep and bring it home.

Notice the number one hundred in this story. In the Bible this number represents wholeness and completeness. When one sheep is lost, the ninety-nine remaining are less than whole. When that one returns, they are whole and complete again, and it's time to celebrate.

All of us have "gone astray like a lost sheep" (Psalm 119:176), but Jesus seeks to gather us in, risking everything to find us and bring us home. As we follow Jesus, we seek others who are lost, so that they might know him. And when they are found, that's cause for celebration! As angels rejoice in heaven when one is found, shouldn't we throw a party in our churches?

What if your congregation became known as a place that welcomes the lost, a place where the lost are found, or as a place that is intentional about reaching out to those outside the church walls? That would be like Luke 15 all over again.

Biblical Wisdom
For the Son of Man came to seek out and to save the lost.
Luke 19:10

Transformative Thought
When things get too complicated, it sometimes makes sense to stop and wonder: Have I asked the right question?[37]
Enrico Bombieri

Silence for Meditation

Psalm Fragment
I have gone astray like a lost sheep; seek out your servant, for I do not forget your commandments.
Psalm 119:176

Questions to Ponder
- Take a few moments to think back on your life. At what times did you feel lost or distant from Jesus? At what times was Jesus searching for you, or gathering you up in his arms?
- What would your congregation need to do to become known as a place that reaches out to those who aren't part of a community of faith? What can you do to help?

Prayer for Today

Amazing grace, how sweet the sound, that saved a wretch like me! I once was lost, but now am found; was blind, but now I see.[38] Thank you, dear Jesus, for seeking me while I was lost, for finding me, and for your amazing grace. In your name I pray. Amen.

Day 28—Saturday
Which of These Was a Neighbor?
Luke 10:25-37

> *"Which of these three, do you think, was a neighbor to the man who fell into the hands of the robbers?"*
> Luke 10:36

Remember Eeyore in *The House at Pooh Corner?*

One day Pooh and Rabbit were dropping Pooh Sticks over the bridge, then running to the other side of the bridge and watching them go by. Again and again they did this. And as they were preparing to drop another stick, they saw Eeyore floating on his back down the river. They asked Eeyore what he was doing.

Eeyore said, "I'll give you three guesses, Rabbit. Digging holes in the ground? Wrong. Leaping from branch to branch of a young oak-tree? Wrong. Waiting for somebody to help me out of the river? Right."[39]

Eeyore was helplessly and hopelessly floating down the river. He couldn't help himself out of the situation. He needed someone to save him from the river's current. Pooh and Rabbit started dropping rocks into the river. Eventually, slowly, the rocks made enough little waves to bring Eeyore to shore.

Jesus tells the story of a man who was beaten and left by the side of the road, helpless and hopeless. A priest and a Levite came along. When they saw the man, they made sure they didn't get too close to him. They walked by on the other side of the road. But a Samaritan, a good Samaritan, stopped, went to the man, bandaged his wounds, took him to an inn, and paid for his care. The Samaritan helped the wounded man out of the "river."

Every day there are people who are floating helplessly and hopelessly down the river of life. Sometimes they don't know how they're going to make it through the day, much less make it through the next week or month. These wounded people are in our paths and all around the world.

The good Samaritan was a neighbor to the man who needed help. He didn't help everyone. That would have been much too big a task. But he did help someone. Jesus says, "Go and do likewise."

Biblical Wisdom
And the king will answer them, "Truly I tell you, just as you did it to one of the least of these who are members of my family, you did it to me."
    Matthew 25:40

Transformative Thought
On the one hand we are called to play the good Samaritan on life's roadside; but that will be only an initial act. One day we must come to see that the whole Jericho Road must be transformed so that men and women will not be constantly beaten and robbed as they make their journey on life's highway. True compassion is more than flinging a coin to a beggar; it is not haphazard and superficial. It comes to see that an edifice which produces beggars needs restructuring.[40]
    Martin Luther King Jr.

Silence for Meditation

Psalm Fragment
For he will hide me in his shelter in the day of trouble; he will conceal me under the cover of his tent; he will set me high on a rock.
    Psalm 27:5

Questions to Ponder
- Who are the people in need today? How could you help one of them?
- It's been said that a congregation is not defined by its *seating* capacity, but by its *sending* capacity. How is your congregation sending people to bind up, help, and heal others in need?

Prayer for Today

Gracious God, open my eyes. Loving Jesus, open my heart. Holy Spirit, open my hands. Direct me, lead me, and guide me to do your will. Help me to see and serve those in need. In Jesus' name. Amen.

Day 29—Monday
Who Is Greater, the One at the Table or the One Who Serves?
Luke 22:24-27

> *"For who is greater, the one who is at the table or the one who serves?"*
> Luke 22:27a

Jesus had just finished sharing his Last Supper with the disciples. He passed around the bread and the wine, saying that this was the new covenant in his blood. He also said that someone sharing that bread and wine—his very body and blood—would soon betray him.

Immediately after this most precious and holy time, a dispute arose among the disciples. They hadn't yet digested the bread, and still had the smell of the wine on their breath. They argued among themselves about which one of them would be the greatest. Unbelievable! Didn't they understand what Jesus had just said and done? How could they be so clueless?

So Jesus asked them, who is greater, someone who is waited on and served at a table, or the person who is serving? If someone else asked this question, the answer would be obvious. But this is Jesus, God's servant, who is about to give up his life for all people. For his followers, servanthood is the way to greatness.

As we walk with Jesus, he calls us to follow his ways of love and servanthood. We love and serve the Lord, and we love and serve other people. We don't love and serve out of duty or obligation, but because Jesus loves and serves us.

Loving and serving others is a difficult path. People can disappoint us. They can be ungrateful. Some may try to take advantage of us. But in the end, love is stronger than hate. Forgiveness is stronger than sin. And life is stronger than death. We know this because of the greatest servant of all, Jesus.

Biblical Wisdom

And whatever you do, in word or deed, do everything in the name of the Lord Jesus, giving thanks to God the Father through him.
    Colossians 3:17

Transformative Thought

Real generosity toward the future lies in giving all to the present.[41]
Albert Camus

Silence for Meditation

Psalm Fragment

For the Lord is high, he regards the lowly. . . . The Lord will fulfill his purpose for me; your steadfast love, O Lord, endures forever. Do not forsake the work of your hands.
    Psalm 138:6, 8

Questions to Ponder

- Think about a time you served without recognition or gratitude from anyone. What did you learn from that experience?
- As you walk with Jesus, how do you follow his ways of loving and serving God and others?

Prayer for Today

Lord Jesus, draw me closer on this walk with you. Help me serve God and others with love. Make me your servant. In your holy name I pray. Amen.

Day 30—Tuesday
What If You Gain the World but Lose Yourself?
    Luke 9:23-27

Then he said to them all, "If any want to become my followers, let them deny themselves and take up their cross daily and follow me. For those who want to save their life will lose it, and those who lose their life for my

*sake will save it. What does it profit them if they gain the whole world, but
lose or forfeit themselves?"*

Luke 9:23-25

As we are finding over and over on this Lenten journey, Jesus doesn't ask easy questions with easy answers. Rather, he asks questions that can transform us and our lives: Are we willing to give our lives for him? Are we willing to take our lives, our priorities, our reputations, and everything we have, and lay it all at the foot of the cross? Are we willing to take up the cross each day and follow him?

It would be easier to follow Jesus if he would stick to easier questions and more "appropriate" topics, don't you think? After all, we've been taught that "if you can't say anything nice, don't say anything at all." If we could domesticate Jesus and rub off his rough edges, he would be more palatable and acceptable. Then he could be our Best Friend Forever, and "like" us on Facebook. That would be nice. But there's nothing "nice" about taking up your cross and dying to your own will and desires.

This week we've looked at life, love, and service, based on Jesus' question, "Do you love me?" When Jesus asked Peter that question, it was an *agape* question: Peter, do you love me with a sacrificial love? Jesus loved and accepted Peter as he was, unconditionally and without reservation. And he loved Peter far too much to let him stay that way. He wanted to lead Peter into a deeper life of discipleship, an *agape* life of taking up his cross and following him every day.

Jesus' question for today calls us to deeper discipleship. What are we spending our lives doing? Are we giving up everything for things that don't last? Are we sacrificing ourselves for things that mean nothing in the end? These aren't "nice" questions, but they call us into a closer walk with Jesus, who has sacrificed everything for us. That's *agape* love.

Take up your cross every day. Love Jesus. Serve others.

Biblical Wisdom

*I give you a new commandment, that you love one another. Just as I have
loved you, you also should love one another.*

John 13:34

Transformative Thought

I believe in Christianity as I believe that the Sun has risen, not only because I see it but because by it I see everything else.[42]

    C. S. Lewis

Silence for Meditation

Psalm Fragment

God is our refuge and strength, a very present help in trouble.

    Psalm 46:1

Questions to Ponder

- Think about something you have given up for the sake of family, friends, home, health, or career. How has this sacrifice affected your life?
- What does it mean in your life to take up your cross each day and follow Jesus?

Prayer for Today

Gracious and loving Lord, you gave up your life for me, yet it is so hard for me to give up my life for you. Give me strength and courage to take up the cross each day. Draw me close on this walk with you. Be with me as I lose my life for your sake and experience your life in me. In your holy name. Amen.

Week Six
How Will You Believe What I Say?

Day 31—Wednesday
How Will You Believe What I Say?

John 5:30-47

> *"If you believed Moses, you would believe me, for he wrote about me. But if you do not believe what he wrote, how will you believe what I say?"*
> John 5:46-47

There must have been times in Jesus' ministry when he wondered what it would take to get through to his disciples. What would it take for them to understand who he really was and what he was sent to earth to do? Why wouldn't they listen? When would they finally understand?

Maybe it was easier for the disciples to believe Jesus after he was crucified, died, and raised to life again. Maybe then they finally understood. This week we will look at five questions—transformative, personal, and empowering questions—that Jesus asked when he appeared to his followers after the resurrection.

Let's set the stage for these questions. Luke 24:13-35 tells the story of two disciples walking on the road from Jerusalem to Emmaus. One is named Cleopas. The other is not even named. These two followers of Jesus were not part of the inner circle of twelve disciples. They were just ordinary people who had followed Jesus.

They were just like us.

In Jerusalem, Cleopas and the other disciple had witnessed the horror of Jesus' crucifixion. They must have believed that his death on the cross was simply the end of the story. In their grief, they felt defeated and deflated, betrayed and let down. They felt like failures because their friend and Lord had been crucified.

Then someone joined them on the road. Though they didn't recognize him at first, when they looked back later they realized that their "hearts burned" as they walked and talked with Jesus.

On the road to Emmaus Jesus gave these two followers vision and direction, new meaning and purpose. Seeing their Lord, now risen from the dead, set their hearts on fire.

How will you believe what Jesus says?

Biblical Wisdom
In Christ we have also obtained an inheritance, having been destined
according to the purpose of him who accomplishes all things according
to his counsel and will.
    Ephesians 1:11

Transformative Thought
So many people walk around with a meaningless life. They seem half-asleep, even when they're busy doing things they think are important. This is because they're chasing the wrong things. The way you get meaning into your life is to devote yourself to loving others, devote yourself to your community around you, and devote yourself to creating something that gives you purpose and meaning.[43]
   Mitch Albom

Silence for Meditation

Psalm Fragment
I cry to God Most High, to God who fulfills his purpose for me.
    Psalm 57:2

Questions to Ponder
- When have you felt like the two disciples on the road to Emmaus, meandering through life without a clear sense of vision and purpose? What did you learn from that experience?
- What would it take for your heart to be set on fire with faith?

Prayer for Today
Dear Jesus, I believe that you died on the cross and were raised to life again. Guide me on the road with you, and help me to follow you all the days of my life. In your holy name. Amen.

Day 32—Thursday
What Are You Discussing with Each Other?
Luke 24:13-17

While they were talking and discussing, Jesus himself came near and went with them, but their eyes were kept from recognizing him. And he said to them, "What are you discussing with each other while you walk along?"
Luke 24:15-17a

Cleopas and an unnamed disciple left Jerusalem and set out on the road toward Emmaus, just seven miles away.

In Jerusalem the one they had followed, the one they had hoped would restore Israel, was put to death on a cross. In Jerusalem they had been shaken to the core and lost their sense of direction. It was a place of disappointment, unmet expectations, tragedy, and loss.

They were on their way to Emmaus. Maybe they just wanted to escape. Maybe they planned to return to the way things were before they met Jesus. Frederick Buechner writes: "Emmaus is whatever we do or wherever we go to make ourselves forget that the world holds nothing sacred, that even the wisest and bravest and loveliest decay and die. . . . Emmaus is where we go, where these two went, to try to forget about Jesus and the great failure of his life."[44]

The two disciples tried to leave behind the horror and tragedy of Jerusalem by escaping to Emmaus. In the middle of all this, Jesus joined the conversation and asked, "What are you talking about?"

Most of us have had times and places like Jerusalem and Emmaus in our lives. In the past, or perhaps even now, everything you believed in has fallen apart. People you trusted have betrayed you. Someone you loved has died. And all you want to do is get away and act like nothing has happened.

In the middle of all this, Jesus is with us. He will not back away when we face difficult times or desert us when we are traveling rough roads. The two disciples had a companion on their journey from Jerusalem to Emmaus. Thank God that you and I do too.

Biblical Wisdom

For I am convinced that neither death, nor life, nor angels, nor rulers, nor things present, nor things to come, nor powers, nor height, nor depth, nor anything else in all creation, will be able to separate us from the love of God in Christ Jesus our Lord.

Romans 8:38-39

Transformative Thought

Maybe you have to know the darkness before you can appreciate the light.[45]
Madeleine L'Engle

Silence for Meditation

Psalm Fragment

Even though I walk through the darkest valley, I fear no evil; for you are with me; your rod and your staff—they comfort me.

Psalm 23:4

Questions to Ponder

- Name a "Jerusalem" in your life, a place or time or event in which you experienced hurt or pain that shook the foundations of your life. Then name an "Emmaus" in your life, a place you go to escape or something you do when you've lost your sense of direction.
- How do you recognize Jesus' presence during your life's journey?

Prayer for Today

Precious Lord, gentle Jesus, sometimes life is really difficult and we lose our sense of direction. At those times, help us recognize your presence in our midst. Join our conversations and walk with us. In your holy name. Amen.

Day 33—Friday
What Things?

Luke 24:17-20

> They stood still, looking sad. Then one of them, whose name was
> Cleopas, answered him, "Are you the only stranger in Jerusalem who
> does not know the things that have taken place there in these days?"
> He asked them, "What things?"
> Luke 24:17b-19a

What would it take to stop you in your tracks on the way from Jerusalem to Emmaus?

The two disciples were talking as they walked along on the way to Emmaus. When a stranger joined them and asked what they were talking about, they stood still. How could he have been in Jerusalem and not know about the things that had happened there?

And so they began to tell him about Jesus, who *was* a prophet, how he *was* condemned and crucified, and how they *had* hoped he would be the one to redeem Israel. Everything they told him was in the past tense. They were living in the past. They were living in an "if only" world, and to be honest, that's very easy to do: *If only* I had been raised differently. *If only* I had a better-paying job or a better education. *If only* I looked great or was more popular. *If only* that person had been who I thought he or she was. *If only* . . . then my life would be so much better.

The two disciples were living in the past. Maybe that's why they didn't recognize Jesus with them in the present moment. And just as Jesus was with them on the road to Emmaus, he is with us on the roads we travel. He is with us on the most difficult paths. He is with us even when we don't recognize him. He is with us right here and right now.

Biblical Wisdom
*"Look, the virgin shall conceive and bear a son, and they shall name him
Emmanuel," which means, "God is with us."*
Matthew 1:23

Transformative Thought
No one is as capable of gratitude as one who has emerged from the kingdom of night.[46]

Elie Wiesel

Silence for Meditation

Psalm Fragment
"Be still, and know that I am God!"
Psalm 46:10

Questions to Ponder

- In your walk with Jesus, what stops you in your tracks or keeps you turning around to look back?
- In what ways is God with you right here and right now?

Prayer for Today

Lord Jesus, walk with us. In our joys and sorrows, walk with us. For today and tomorrow, walk with us. In your holy name. Amen.

Day 34—Saturday
Was It Not Necessary?

Luke 24:21-35

Then he said to them, "Oh, how foolish you are, and how slow of heart to believe all that the prophets have declared! Was it not necessary that the Messiah should suffer these things and then enter into his glory?"
Luke 24:25-26

Many people we regard highly today were at some point considered failures. Wolfgang Mozart was told by Emperor Ferdinand that his opera *The Marriage of Figaro* was far too noisy and contained too many notes. Vincent Van Gogh sold only one painting in his lifetime. Thomas Edison was considered unteachable as a young child. Albert Einstein was told by a teacher that he would never amount to much.

Looking back on what had happened in Jerusalem, the two disciples on the road to Emmaus must have seen Jesus as a failure. They had hoped that he would redeem and restore Israel, but in the end he suffered and died on a cross like a common criminal. They were not the only ones who had difficulty with this. The apostle Paul pointed out that the crucified Christ was a "stumbling block" and "foolishness" for many. For those who believe, however, he said the crucified Christ shows "the power of God and the wisdom of God" (1 Corinthians 1:23-24).

In his theology of the cross, Martin Luther described how God's power, wisdom, and glory are shown most fully in things that appear weak, foolish, and lowly. For example, God's word took on flesh and blood in a baby born in a manger. On the cross, God's Son died an excruciating death. Now all who believe in Jesus raised from the dead receive new life and continue to proclaim Christ crucified.

Biblical Wisdom
We proclaim Christ crucified, a stumbling block to Jews and foolishness to Gentiles, but to those who are the called, both Jews and Greeks, Christ the power of God and the wisdom of God.
    1 Corinthians 1:23-24

Transformative Thought
Now it is not sufficient for anyone, and it does him no good to recognize God in his glory and majesty, unless he recognizes him in the humility and shame of the cross.[47]
Martin Luther

Silence for Meditation

Psalm Fragment
The LORD is my rock, my fortress, and my deliverer, my God, my rock in whom I take refuge, my shield, and the horn of my salvation, my stronghold.
    Psalm 18:2

- How do you look at Jesus' suffering and death on the cross? In other words, what does the cross mean to you?
- In what ways does your congregation proclaim Christ crucified?

Prayer for Today

Gracious God, I am in awe of the power, wisdom, and glory you revealed on the cross. Renew my hope, my faith, and my life, through Jesus Christ, my Savior and Lord. Amen.

Day 35—Monday
Why Do You Doubt?
Luke 24:36-40

> *He said to them, "Why are you frightened, and why do doubts arise in your hearts?"*
> Luke 24:38

We all have doubts. We have doubts about other people: Can we trust that group? What's the hidden agenda here? We have doubts about the future: Will the world ever experience peace? Will we be secure? We have doubts about our decisions: Did we do the right things? Did we make the right choices? We have doubts about ourselves: Are we qualified to do this? How could God love us? And we have doubts about God: Is the good news about Jesus too good to be true? Where is God when people we love suffer and die?

The disciples had doubts too. After Jesus broke bread with the two disciples who had been on the way to Emmaus, they recognized him and were overjoyed. They were so excited that they went back to Jerusalem to tell the Eleven (the twelve chosen by Jesus, minus Judas) what had happened. Everyone was talking when Jesus stood in their midst. Suddenly they were all afraid. Jesus asked them, "Why are you frightened, and why do doubts arise in your hearts?" Then he showed them the scars from the wounds in his hands and feet, and invited them to touch him so they could see that it was him standing there and not a ghost. As Luke's Gospel ends, Jesus is teaching and blessing this group.

Sometimes when we have doubts, we think our faith isn't good enough. Maybe it's just too frail and weak. We're afraid other people will find out about the doubt we have buried deep inside ourselves. Maybe the church and faith are not for us. But at these times, remember where Jesus was when the disciples had doubts—right there with them.

Jesus is right here with us too, in the midst of doubt, fear, and pain, and in the midst of faith, joy, and praise. He invites us to see and feel the cool baptismal waters, to take the bread and eat it, and to drink the wine. He teaches us and blesses us and helps us to grow in faith as we walk with him.

Don't underestimate the power of a mustard seed of faith. No matter how weak or frail you think your faith is, it is enough, because Jesus is with you. You don't need faith the size of a mountain to move a mustard seed. You need faith the size of a mustard seed to move a mountain.

Biblical Wisdom
But ask in faith, never doubting, for the one who doubts is like a wave of the sea, driven and tossed by the wind.
　　James 1:6

Transformative Thought
I have a lot of faith. But I am also afraid a lot, and have no real certainty about anything. I remembered something Father Tom had told me—that the opposite of faith is not doubt, but certainty. Certainty is missing the point entirely. Faith includes noticing the mess, the emptiness and discomfort, and letting it be there until some light returns.[48]
　　Anne Lamott

Silence for Meditation

Psalm Fragment
Fools say in their hearts, "There is no God."
　　Psalm 14:1

Questions to Ponder

- Where and when is it okay to express your doubts about God or faith?
- What role, if any, does doubt play in your walk with Jesus?

Prayer for Today

Faithful God, I want to believe. Help me with my disbelief and doubt. By your Spirit, help me to know you, trust you, and grow in faith each day. Let me see you and experience your presence. This I pray in Jesus' name. Amen.

Day 36—Tuesday
Do You Have Anything to Eat?
Luke 24:41-53

While in their joy they were disbelieving and still wondering, he said to them, "Have you anything here to eat?"
Luke 24:41

The disciples' doubt and fear began to turn to joy and wonder. Just then Jesus asked them for something to eat. When they gave him a piece of fish, he took it and ate it.

There are so many things Luke might have written at this point. The Gospel he wrote is about to end. In the course of Jesus' ministry, he must have eaten with the disciples countless times. Why does Luke bother to include anything about Jesus eating broiled fish?

Maybe Jesus simply was hungry. At any rate, he ate the piece of fish right in front of the disciples. Only if Jesus was real and alive could he get hungry and eat. Maybe that's why Luke includes two sentences about this little snack. In the simple, ordinary act of eating, Jesus shows the disciples that he's real and he's alive!

Jesus is real and alive. But do we truly believe this? Maybe we know a lot *about* Jesus but don't know *him* in our daily lives. Maybe we talk on Sundays about Jesus as if he is real and alive but not during the rest of the week. What would happen if we truly believed and acted like Jesus is real and alive in the world today, in our congregations, and in our lives? What would each day look like then?

Jesus is real and alive, and that makes this a Holy Week indeed.

Biblical Wisdom
"For 'In him we live and move and have our being.'"
    Acts 17:28a

Transformative Thought
Asking the proper question is the central action of transformation. . . . Questions are the keys that cause the secret doors of the psyche to swing open.[49]
Clarissa Pinkola Estes

Silence for Meditation

Psalm Fragment
Commit your way to the LORD; trust in him, and he will act.
    Psalm 37:5

Questions to Ponder
- Think of someone you know for whom Jesus seems very real and alive. What does this person's life and faith look like?
- Where do you see Jesus' real, living presence during this Holy Week?

Prayer for Today
Lord Jesus, you are the Son of God. You are real. You are alive. Draw me closer to you. In your name I pray. Amen.

Week Seven
Whom Are You Looking For?

Day 37—Wednesday
Whom Are You Looking For?

John 20:11-18

When she had said this, she turned around and saw Jesus standing
there, but she did not know that it was Jesus. Jesus said to her, "Woman,
why are you weeping? Whom are you looking for?"
John 20:14-15a

Our first week on this transformative journey through Lent began with the question "What are you looking for?" That week ended with Jesus' question to the soldiers and police who had come to arrest him: "Whom are you looking for?"

Today Jesus asks that question again, but in very different circumstances. Mary Magdalene was at his tomb early on Sunday morning, weeping and wailing. She was devastated and brokenhearted. She was so upset that when Jesus asked, "Woman, why are you weeping? Whom are you looking for?" she believed he was the gardener and asked where Jesus' body had been taken.

But then something amazing happened. Jesus said to her, "Mary." And she turned and recognized him. Jesus spoke her name, and she turned and came face-to-face with the living Lord, Savior, Messiah, Son of God. When Jesus spoke her name, she realized he was standing right in front of her.

In this final week of our Lenten journey, turn and face Jesus, and hear him speak your name. He knows you and loves you and gave his life for you. He has kept you close throughout your life. No struggles, no problems, no sins, nothing in your past can separate you from his love.

Jesus is the one you've been looking for all along.

Biblical Wisdom
Moses said to the Lᴏʀᴅ, ". . . Yet you have said, 'I know you by name, and
you have also found favor in my sight.' "
Exodus 33:12

Transformative Thought

Love costs all we are
and will ever be.
Yet it is only love
which sets us free.[50]
  Maya Angelou

Silence for Meditation

Psalm Fragment
Those who love me, I will deliver; I will protect those who know my name.
  Psalm 91:14

Questions to Ponder
- Before Jesus spoke Mary's name, she mistook him for the gardener. What do people mistake Jesus for today?
- When have you turned to face Jesus or heard him "speak your name"? How did this affect your life?

Prayer for Today

Holy Jesus, you know me better than I know myself. Thank you for loving me and calling me your own. In your most holy name. Amen.

Day 38—Thursday
Do You Know What I Have Done for You?
  John 13:1-20

After he had washed their feet, had put on his robe, and had returned to the table, he said to them, "Do you know what I have done to you?"
  John 13:12

Imagine walking on dusty roads to get to someone's home. When you arrive, the homeowner hands you a bowl of water. You take off your sandals and wash your grimy feet, or your host has someone ready to wash your feet.

This was a common practice in Jesus' time. Household servants or slaves, rather than homeowners, would perform the lowly, menial task of washing feet. In some cases, followers of a teacher would wash the teacher's feet.

How could the disciples know or understand what Jesus was doing when he took on this task? Having their Lord and Teacher stoop to wash their feet was shocking. No wonder Simon Peter at first refused when Jesus came to him with the water basin and towel!

After he finished washing the disciples' feet, Jesus returned to his seat. He explained that this was an example for all of them. As he had washed their feet, they should wash one another's feet.

What might it mean for us today to treat others the way Jesus has treated us? How will we follow his example, wash feet, and serve as he served?

Biblical Wisdom

Let the same mind be in you that was in Christ Jesus, who, though he was in the form of God, did not regard equality with God as something to be exploited, but emptied himself, taking the form of a slave, being born in human likeness.
Philippians 2:5-7

Transformative Thought

Humility is the mother of all virtues; purity, charity and obedience. It is in being humble that our love becomes real, devoted, and ardent.[51]
Mother Teresa

Silence for Meditation

Psalm Fragment

Make me to know your ways, O LORD; teach me your paths.
Psalm 25:4

Questions to Ponder

- If you had been among the twelve disciples, how would you have reacted to Jesus washing your feet?

- What might it mean for you and your congregation to wash feet and serve as Jesus served?

Prayer for Today

Lord Jesus, as you served, help me to serve others. As you loved, help me to love others. As you lead, help me to follow. In your holy name I pray. Amen.

Day 39—Friday
My God, My God, Why Have You Forsaken Me?
Mark 15:33-37

At three o'clock Jesus cried out with a loud voice, "Eloi, Eloi, lema sabach-thani?" which means, "My God, my God, why have you forsaken me?"
Mark 15:34

It's a cry of abandonment and utter aloneness: "My God, my God, why have you forsaken me?" Some call it the "cry of dereliction." It's the cry of Jesus from the cross.

This cry also appears in Psalm 22. The psalmist felt that with all the tragedies in his life, God must have disowned or abandoned him.

Maybe you've felt like this too. As a pastor, I've talked with many people dealing with the loss of a loved one, the loss of a marriage, or the loss of a job. I often say that feeling deep pain and sadness—and feeling abandoned by God—is normal in situations like these. God created us to feel things passionately.

When we feel like God is nowhere to be found, in the darkest times of our lives, Jesus shows us what to do. In Jesus' darkest hour, as he was suffering and dying on the cross, he cried out to God. He clung to God even when he felt God was not there.

Jesus cried out to God, and we can do the same, with all of our pain and sadness and sense of abandonment. When you feel like God is nowhere to be found, in the darkest times of your life, Jesus knows what this feels like. Cling to him, cling to God. You are never alone. As you cry out to God, Jesus is there with you.

Biblical Wisdom
Jesus began to weep.
John 11:35

Transformative Thought
There is no pit so deep that God's love is not deeper still.[52]
Corrie ten Boom

Silence for Meditation

Psalm Fragment
Posterity will serve him; future generations will be told about the Lord, and proclaim his deliverance to a people yet unborn, saying that he has done it.
Psalm 22:30-31

Questions to Ponder
- Think about a time you felt lost, alone, or abandoned by God. What was it like? What helped you through that time?
- Jesus cried out to God, and he is with you when you cry out to God out of pain, sadness, or a sense of abandonment. What thoughts or feelings do you have about this?

Prayer for Today
Loving God, sometimes I feel so lost and alone and abandoned. Sometimes it feels like you aren't there. During these times, help me cling to you and cling to Jesus. Help me pour out my pain, sadness, and grief as I cry out to you. Remind me that you are always with me and will never leave me. In Jesus' name. Amen.

Day 40—Saturday
Have You Believed Because You Have Seen Me?

John 20:19-29

> Then he said to Thomas, "Put your finger here and see my hands. Reach
> out your hand and put it in my side. Do not doubt but believe." Thomas
> answered him, "My Lord and my God!" Jesus said to him, "Have you
> believed because you have seen me? Blessed are those who have not
> seen and yet have come to believe."
>
> John 20:27-29

The disciples were hiding behind locked doors when Jesus appeared, risen from
the dead. He greeted them with peace and showed them the scars in his hands
and side. The disciples were overjoyed.

But Thomas wasn't there when this happened. When the other disciples told
him they had seen the risen Lord, he said, "Unless I see the mark of the nails in
his hands, and put my finger in the mark of the nails and my hand in his side, I
will not believe" (John 20:25). In other words, *seeing is believing*. Many of us, like
Thomas, want to believe, but first we want to see for ourselves. Just give us some
proof, we say.

Jesus came to the disciples again. This time Thomas was there, and Jesus
spoke directly to him. Go ahead, look at my hands. Reach out and touch my side.
Then Thomas said, "My Lord and my God!" Jesus asked, "Have you believed
because you have seen me? Blessed are those who have not seen and yet have
come to believe."

This blessing from Jesus is for all of us who have not physically seen him but
believe. "Seeing is believing" is true in many cases, but when it comes to faith,
believing is seeing. Believing is seeing the presence of Jesus with us on the journey
through life. On all the detours, in the midst of the mess, and everywhere we go,
Jesus is there. Believing is seeing and experiencing him as he heals, strengthens,
and guides us. Believing is beginning to see things differently, beginning to see
how God is active in our lives and in the world. Jesus is with us every step along
the way, leading, guiding, encouraging, and strengthening us for life's journey—
beyond question!

Biblical Wisdom

For to this you have been called, because Christ also suffered for you, leaving you an example, so that you should follow in his steps.

1 Peter 2:21

Transformative Thought

It is not the answer that enlightens, but the question.[53]

Eugéne Ionesco

Silence for Meditation

Psalm Fragment

I believe that I shall see the goodness of the Lord in the land of the living.

Psalm 27:13

Questions to Ponder

- List three things you've learned as you've worked through Jesus' questions.
- What you have come to believe during this Lenten journey? How might you share this with someone else?

Prayer for Today

Thank you, Lord Jesus, for all you have done. Thank you for leading me into deeper discipleship through your questions. Help me believe. Help me see. And always draw me close to you. Thank you, Lord Jesus, for everything. Amen.

Notes

1   *Luther's Works*, ed. Jaroslav Pelikan, Helmut T. Lehman, and Hilton C. Oswald, 55 vols. (Philadelphia: Fortress Press; St. Louis: Concordia, 1955–1986), "A Simple Way to Pray" (1535), 43:198.

2   In John Dear, *The Questions of Jesus: Challenging Ourselves to Discover Life's Great Answers* (New York: Doubleday, 2001), preface.

3   *God Has a Dream: A Vision of Hope for Our Time* (Colorado Springs: Image, 2005).

4   *Here and Now: Living in the Spirit*, 10th ed. (New York: Crossroad, 2006).

5   Paraphrased from Lewis Carroll, *Alice's Adventures in Wonderland* (originally published in 1864).

6   *The Following of Christ*, 3rd ed. (Independence, KY: Gale Eighteenth Century Collections Online, 2010).

7   ELW, p. 22.

8   *Alcoholics Anonymous*, 4th ed. (New York: Alcoholics Anonymous World Services, 2001), 417.

9   Reinhold Niebuhr, "Serenity Prayer," adapted by Alcoholics Anonymous.

10   *The Return of the Prodigal Son: A Story of Homecoming* (London: Darton Longman and Todd, 1994).

11   *Mere Christianity* (San Francisco: HarperSanFrancisco, 2001).

12   In *Christianity Today* (online), November 22, 2010.

13   *Sermones* 4.1.1.

14 Evening Vespers, *Lutheran Book of Worship* (Minneapolis: Augsburg Publishing House; Philadelphia: Board of Publication, Lutheran Church in America, 1978), 153.

15 *Confessions*, I, 1.

16 *Celebration of Discipline: The Path to Spiritual Growth*, 3rd ed. (San Francisco: HarperSanFrancisco, 1988), 6.

17 *Ten Times One Is Ten* (1870).

18 *The Modern Review*, October 1941.

19 "Let Us Ever Walk with Jesus," ELW 802, stanza 1.

20 *Riverside Sermons* (New York: Harper & Brothers, 1958), 22.

21 Paraphrase of Felix Mendelssohn, *Psalm 40:1, Hymn of Praise: No. 5, I waited for the Lord.*

22 *The World* (1629).

23 Foreword in Frederic and Mary Ann Brussat, *Spiritual Literacy: Reading the Sacred in Everyday Life* (New York: Touchstone, 1996), 10.

24 Adapted from "On Courage," *Chicken Soup for the Soul*, written and compiled by Jack Canfield and Mark Victor Hansen (Deerfield Beach, FL: Health Communications, Inc.), 27–28.

25 *The Autobiography of Martin Luther King, Jr.*, ed. Clayborne Carson (New York: Grand Central Publishing, 2001).

26 *Back to Methuselah* (1921), part 1, act 1.

27 *The Secret Life of Bees* (New York: Penguin, 2003).

28 "Interview to the Press," in *Young India* (April 2, 1931), reprinted in *Collected Works of Mahatma Gandhi Online*, vol. 51.

29 *Everyday Grace* (New York: Riverhead Trade, 2004), 120.

30 "Blest Be the Tie That Binds," ELW 656, stanza 1.

31 *On Liberty* (New York: Cosimo Classics, 2005), first published 1859.

32 In "Arun Gandhi Shares the Mahatma's Message," by Michel W. Potts, *India—West*, 27, no. 13 (February 1, 2002), A34.

33 *The Inner Life* (London: Penguin UK, 2005).

34 ELW, p. 34.

35 *Traveling Mercies: Some Thoughts on Faith* (New York: Knopf Doubleday, 2000).

36 "Jesus Loves Me!," ELW 595, stanza 1 and refrain.

37 "Prime Territory," *The Sciences* (September/October 1992), 30–36.

38 "Amazing Grace, How Sweet the Sound," ELW 779, stanza 1.

39 A. A. Milne, *The World of Pooh* (New York: E. P. Dutton, 1957), 240.

40 "A Time to Break Silence," speech delivered April 4, 1967, Riverside Church, New York City.

41 *The Rebel* (New York: Vintage, 1992).

42 "Is Theology Poetry?" in *They Asked for a Paper* (London: Geoffrey Bles, 1962).

43 *Tuesdays with Morrie* (New York: Broadway, 2002).

44 *The Magnificent Defeat* (New York: HarperCollins, 1985).

45 *A Ring of Endless Light* (New York: Macmillan, 1980).

46 Nobel acceptance speech (December 10, 1986).

47 Heidelberg Disputation, *Martin Luther's Basic Theological Writings*, ed. Timothy F. Lull, 2nd ed. (Minneapolis: Fortress, 2005), 57.

48 *Plan B: Further Thoughts on Faith* (New York: Riverhead Trade, 2006).

49 *Women Who Run with the Wolves: Myths and Stories of the Wild Woman Archetype* (New York: Ballantine, 1992).

50 From "A Brave and Startling Truth," written for the 50th anniversary of the United Nations, 1995.

51   *In the Heart of the World: Thoughts, Stories and Prayers* (Novato, CA: New World Library, 1997).

52   *The Hiding Place* (Grand Rapids, MI: Chosen Books, 2006).

53   *Découvertes* (Paris: Albert Skira, 1969).